The Elements of
Grammar
90 in Minutes

The Elements of
Grammar
90 in Minutes

Robert Hollander

Dover Publications, Inc.
Mineola, New York

For Justice Stephen Breyer, whose remarks about the parts of speech, made a few years ago, spurred me to write this little book.

Bibliographical Note

The Elements of Grammar in 90 Minutes is a new work, first published by Dover Publications, Inc., in 2011.

Library of Congress Cataloging-in-Publication Data

Hollander, Robert, 1933–
The elements of grammar in 90 minutes / Robert Hollander.
    p. cm.
  ISBN-13: 978-0-486-48114-2
  ISBN-10: 0-486-48114-X
  1. English language—Grammar. 2. English language—Grammar—Problems, exercises, etc. I. Title.
  PE1112.H627 2011
  428.0076—dc22

2010052826

Manufactured in the United States by Courier Corporation
48114X01
www.doverpublications.com

ACKNOWLEDGMENTS

All parents know what a pleasure it is to acknowledge a debt to one's own children. Both Zaz and Buzz agreed to be guinea pigs, reading drafts of this book with helpful suggestions for amendment, thus revealing—yet again—just how wise I was when I chose their mother.

I would like also to thank my friend Sevilla de Guzman, a Philippine-American and thus representative of one group of people whom I hope this book will serve, those who have come to this country without the benefit of a formal introduction to English grammar and who feel its lack. Sevilla was the first "external" reader of this book and I learned a lot from her reactions.

John Beall, head of the English Department at Collegiate School, on the Upper West Side of Manhattan (where, in addition to his more expected commitments, he regularly teaches his eighth-grade students how to read Dante's *Commedia*), offered a series of useful comments, some of which are reflected in this final draft.

My friend John Angus McPhee has not only furnished many examples of our language working at its best, but has helped shape the conception of this book; a pupil whom he and I shared at Princeton University, David Remnick, now known for much more than for those who taught him, has also offered helpful advice.

My largest debt is to David Phillips. I first met David when I was twenty-two and he twelve, a seventh-grader in one of the first English classes I taught after I graduated from college, at Collegiate School. I still remember with awe some of his accomplishments as a young reader and writer. We both left Collegiate for "greener pastures" and I lost track of him until, in the fall of 2009, the alumni news from Collegiate contained a note from him. A few e-mails later, I told him that I had been working on this book about English grammar and felt that I needed help putting it into better shape. The present form of the text is chiefly the result of his intervention. I am most grateful to him.

TABLE OF CONTENTS

Preface: *The Reason for This Book*   1

Introduction: *About Grammar*   7

Part I: *The Parts of Speech*   11
  Nouns and Pronouns   12
  Verbs   15
  Adjectives (and Articles)   20
  Adverbs   23
  Conjunctions   24
  Prepositions   27
  Interjections   28
  Verbals   29

Part II: *The Sentence*   34
  Subject, Object, and Predicate   35
  Clauses and Phrases   37
  Kinds of Sentences   37

Part III: *Some Practical Considerations Bridging
Grammar and Usage*   40
  Agreement (person, number, case, and gender)   41
  Split Infinitives   51

The Subjunctive Mood   55
Levels of Discourse: 58
    (1) *who* or *whom?*   62
    (2) *like* or *as?*   65
    (3) *between* or *among?*   66
    (4) *due to* or *because of?*   67
    (5) *which* or *that?*   69
    (6) Dangling prepositions   71
    (7) Nouns used as adjectives   72

Part IV: *Analyzing Sentences*   75
A Paragraph from the Wild   75
Diagramming Sentences   83

Index of Terms   84

Appendix   87

PREFACE: THE REASON FOR THIS BOOK

This book offers instruction in the basic rules of English grammar. It is offered to those in need of such assistance, either because they were never taught these rules or because they have forgotten what they once were taught. I am aware that the person reading this probably has many competing projects alongside a desire to know English grammar better. Thus, at the outset, let me make you this promise: If you put ninety minutes of your full attention into this short book, you will gain at least a working sense of the basics of English grammar. I hope the investment that you have made in acquiring it (and plan to make in studying it) will *at least* be matched by an improvement in your understanding of our common language.

My purpose is not theoretical but practical. Further, this is not a work about stylistics, like Strunk and White's *The Elements of Style*. While there are many such aids and while consideration of stylistic choices is a useful adjunct to the study of grammar, my central concern is grammar itself. This is also not a reference work concerning the refinements of speaking and writing. Many of these are also already available. My aim is different—to offer a basic understanding of English grammar conceived as *the logical arrangement of the parts of a sentence*—in other words, the building blocks of the English language.

This subject has by common consent (in America anyway) been largely banished from study and even from conversation, except for a random presence in scattered classrooms, many of them devoted to the teaching of *foreign* languages. Some of us only learned the grammar of our own language when we happened to study a language other than our own. That's how I learned, quite some time ago in high school, since my grammar school, a so-called progressive school, had banned grammar from its curriculum as a matter of educational policy.

The idea for this project came out of my experience at a "Renaissance Weekend" in Charleston, South Carolina, in December 2005. In an exchange with another panelist, I pointed out that the word *grammar* was rarely or never heard in politicians' frequent references to the problems of American education. Although we often hear our elected representatives speak about this "crisis," I said, we never hear them mention that millions of our fellow citizens know very little about the rules that govern our use of language—that is to say, grammar. Some years ago, I continued, I asked a class of Princeton students what St. Augustine and his fellow fourth-century students of Latin learned when they studied grammar. No one in that wood-paneled room knew; I explained that those young North African students were first taught the parts of speech.

How many of these are there, I asked? Several guessed, but no one knew. When I tried to have the members of the class identify them one at a time, they came up short again. Eventually I had to introduce these college students to the traditional eight parts of speech. And I also told them that their ignorance—shocking though it was in students at a celebrated American university—was not their fault but ours, the adults in charge of their education.

As I began writing this book, I decided to test my sense of the political isolation of grammar by searching the *Congressional Record* for 2007. By July of that year its database already contained over 11,000,000 words in 10,400 documents. The word *education* occurred 11,199 times in 1,810 documents, but *grammar* only 13 times (in 11 documents). Of those 13, nine appeared in the phrase *grammar school*, which has come to mean a school where grammar is no longer taught. And most of those nine were not even about education, but were just the names of schools certain people happened to have attended. In all those words there was only one mention of grammar as important to education—in a speech by Senator Thad Cochran (R-Miss.) supporting reauthorization of the National Writing Project. He said:

> Writing skills for employment in the 21st century require not only the grammar, construction and analytical thought of traditional writing, but the skills needed to communicate effectively using new technology.

If I was wrong back there in South Carolina, I was not wrong by very much. In all those Congressional hours of discussion, debate, gilded rhetoric, and heartfelt pleading, in all that time spent lamenting the neglected condition of American education, it was said only once that people need to know grammar in order to write effectively. Most American children are no longer learning to use this basic and important tool, and thus are deprived of what is—or should be—their birthright.

It was not always so; it need not remain so. Grammar could (and should) be put back into the grade-school curriculum in a meaningful way. What used to be called *English* is now often referred to as *Language Arts*, yet these do not include a serious study of what, some sixteen centuries ago, was called "the first art." Grammar helps us clarify our thoughts, control our own writing and speech, and avoid error (including the sometimes paralyzing fear of error). Knowing grammar helps enable the close study of written texts, not only literary texts but any writings (for example, contracts) that require analysis. Grammar is essential for editing one's own and others' writing; further, it assists our study of other languages.

This book offers those who missed out on grammar in school (or who may not remember it as clearly as they might wish) a chance to learn or relearn its fundamentals now. It is never too late, the investment is small, and the advantage is potentially large indeed. Further, you may find yourself enjoying the experience.

After an Introduction about grammar itself, this book is divided into four parts:

The first is about the parts of speech—classifying words according to their use in a sentence.

The second studies the process by which words form a coherent sentence.

The third offers observations bridging grammar and usage.

The fourth analyzes the structure of an exemplary paragraph.

INTRODUCTION: ABOUT GRAMMAR

The origins of grammar are hidden in a mysterious past. Somewhere between grunting and speaking came its first glimmerings. Every language has a grammar of its own, an internal structure, something like its skeleton. As is also true of animals and their skeletons, the grammar of every language changes slowly over time as the language evolves and mutates. Closely related languages tend to have similar grammatical structures, while unrelated languages may have vastly different ones.

Grammar is intrinsic to all languages. The *study* of a language's grammar must be consciously and deliberately performed. The development of writing, with the consequent need to codify usage, encouraged such study. The discipline of linguistics has by now described the formal grammar of most languages.

Scholars agree that Greek was the first European language whose grammar was studied as a subject in itself, sometime around 500 B.C.E. (Sanskrit grammars began appearing in India at about the same time). The Romans applied the principles of Greek grammar to their own language, Latin, which was related but in many ways quite different (for example, there are verb forms in Greek that do not occur in Latin). As Latin transformed over time into the so-called *Romance* languages (principally French, Italian, Portuguese, Spanish and Romanian), these preserved its grammar in varying degrees.

English was at first a *Teutonic* language, brought to England during the Germanic invasions which began in the fifth century C.E., after the collapse of Roman power in Britain. It shared a common Indo-European origin with Greek and Latin, and some Latin words were acquired before the invasions, but its grammar and most of its vocabulary were quite different. This *Old English*, sometimes called *Anglo-Saxon* after the names of two of the invading peoples, became the language of England and remained so until the Norman Conquest in 1066. Latin was forgotten and the Celtic languages of the earlier inhabitants were displaced into marginal territories. With the Norman Conquest a new ruling class was introduced into England; it spoke Norman French, a Romance language. The two languages merged into what we now call *Middle English*, which still preserved many Germanic forms (*holpen*, says Chaucer, instead of *helped*). Standardization of dialect and the introduction of printing helped change this transitional tongue into modern English. The work of Chaucer, who died in 1400, can now be read in its original form only after considerable study. Within a little over a century after the introduction of printing in England (1476), we see texts like Shakespeare's plays (which began to appear around 1590) and the King James Bible (completed in 1611), which are still read, understood, and enjoyed in their original form 400 years later.

In medieval and later pre-modern Europe (until about 1800), Latin was the language of all educated people and the *lingua franca* of the professionals of the day: clergymen, teachers, politicians, doctors, and lawyers. Latin became normative because it was the language in which all European schooling was offered. As a result, English grammar was first studied and its elements classified according to the categories of Latin grammar, even though these were only imperfectly adapted to the hybrid English speech. Like it or not, all English speakers have this common linguistic heritage. Grammar books about English were not produced until at least the sixteenth century; the flowering of English grammar as a subject of study did not occur until the eighteenth century.

Because English grammar was understood through the prism of Latin, those who made the first deliberate rules for English writing and speech went out of their way to make their language conform to Latin usage. The current (and necessary) dispute between *descriptive* grammarians ("whatever people actually say or write is acceptable") and *prescriptive* grammarians ("people ought to know and observe the established rules") is driven to some degree by the incongruities between "pure" Latin grammar (what the Prescriptors long for in English) and English actuality (what the Descriptors love about the unruly vitality of our spoken language). Now that Latin is no longer a spoken language, we may call its grammatical structures and rules fixed; English, like all other living languages, is always changing. This is not a disadvantage—the mutability of English helps explain its attractiveness to both speakers and writers.

The Prescriptors are clearly wrong about the applicability of some Latin rules to English practice, but the Descriptors perhaps go too far toward a belief that any form of expression is as valuable as any other, thus opening very wide the gates to acceptable expression. Hard, firm rules make things easier, while do-what-you-will permissiveness tends to leave us perplexed. Tradition-based grammar can be boiled down fairly easily, while "anything goes" systems are disorganized, even chaotic. But the Descriptors are right in the long run—Latin is no longer changing, but English is. If it had not changed, we might all still speak "Chaucerian," a language now so distant from modern forms that most people need a translation to read it. In what follows, we will try to negotiate a path between these two positions.

PART I: THE PARTS OF SPEECH

The most influential of the early formulators of Latin grammar, Aelius Donatus, wrote toward the close of the fourth century. His *Ars Minor*, which dealt with the parts of speech, was the essential school text for most European boys in their Latin schools (and some wealthy girls in their homes) from the Middle Ages until the late sixteenth century. Donatus' grammar begins:

> How many are the parts of speech? Eight. What are they? Noun, pronoun, verb, adverb, participle, conjunction, preposition, interjection.

Except that what Donatus called a *participle* we call an *adjective*—otherwise his terms are identical with those we use today.

Why is it important to know the parts of speech? Because with them we can divide a language with hundreds of thousands of words (perhaps a million if we include all specialized vocabularies of contemporary English) into eight categories of function. With these few easily mastered categories, we can begin to understand the structure of any sentence, see whether it is working correctly, and repair it if it is not.

The generally accepted names of the parts of English speech are:

Noun	**Adverb**
Pronoun	**Preposition**
Verb	**Conjunction**
Adjective	**Interjection**

NOUNS AND PRONOUNS

A ***noun*** (from the Latin *nomen*, a name) is the name of a person (**Harold**), a place (**Chicago**), a thing (**shovel**), or a concept (**justice**).

Names, usually capitalized, are called ***proper nouns***.

I like *Ike*.

It is hot every summer in *Mississippi*.

A ***pronoun*** functions exactly like a noun. It is a word, usually of few letters, that replaces a noun, usually to avoid repetition.

Bart walks across the stage, scowling at *me* as *he* crosses *it*.

I give *him* a wave.

He seems unaware of *me*.

I can see that *he* wants to give his speech.

Nouns and pronouns identify the actors who perform or receive the actions in a sentence (*I* and *him* in the second sentence), or who exist in the state of being the sentence describes (*He* in the third sentence; in the fourth sentence *his* is not used as a pronoun, but as an adjective).

Pronouns like *I* and *him* are **personal pronouns**, but there are other kinds of pronouns too, including:

Reflexive (Helen pinched *herself*.)
Demonstrative (*These* are my people.)
Interrogative (*Whose* people are these?)
Relative (He's the man *who* can do the job.)
Expletive (*It* is a lovely day.) (Note that the pronoun here does not stand for a noun but serves only a formal introductory purpose.)

Pronouns vary their form by **person** and **number**. There are six *persons* (not *people*) in English: first-, second-, and third-person *singular*, and first-, second-, and third-person *plural*.

The first-person singular is the speaker: I.
The second-person singular is the person whom the speaker is addressing: you.
The third-person singular is anyone or anything else: he, she, it (referring to "Fred" or "Ginger" or "sandwich").
The first-person plural includes the speaker, but also others: we.
The second-person plural includes all whom the speaker is addressing. This is also you.

The third-person plural is anyone or anything else, but more than one: they (referring to "Fred and Ginger" or "soup and sandwich").

As noted, in modern English the second-person singular and plural are identical: *you*. This can be confusing, as sometimes it is not clear from context which one is meant.

When I called last week, *you* told me my order would be ready.

Does the speaker mean *the specific person to whom he or she is speaking* (you singular) or *the company* (a collective used as a plural)? Sometimes it is necessary to explain this ambiguity. It was not always so; the second-person singular used to be *thou* (with the related forms *thy, thee, thyself, thine*), which distinguished it from the plural.

Pronouns also vary by **case**: *subjective, possessive, objective*. For more about case, see page 42.

I, mine, me
you [singular], yours, you
he, his, him; she, hers, her; it, its, it
we, ours, us
you [plural], yours, you
they, theirs, them

As will become clear, these six persons also are linked to the varying forms of verbs.

VERBS

A *verb* is a word that conveys either the action performed by a noun or pronoun, or that noun's (or pronoun's) state of being. Verbs are thus either *verbs of action* or *verbs of state*.

He *hissed* at the countess, who *was* calm at first and then *became* angry, but *said* nothing. (*Hissed* and *said* are verbs of action; *was* and *became* are verbs of state.)

Verbs of action have two *voices*: the *active voice*, in which the subject acts, and the *passive voice*, in which the subject is acted upon.

Active: We *appreciated* the silence.

Passive: The silence *was appreciated*.

Verbs of state show how someone or something seems or feels.

The sea *was* calm and the sky *seemed* its blue mirror.

Her touch *felt* soft, but her voice *was* edgy.

As nouns change their form by number, from singular to plural, and pronouns change by person and case as well as number, the forms of verbs also change, varying with respect to *person*, *tense*, *voice*, *mood*, and *aspect*. Change in form, in nouns and verbs alike, is called *inflection*; the act of inflecting verbs is called *conjugation*; inflection of nouns, pronouns, and adjectives is called *declension*.

The basic conjugation of a verb lists the variations by *person*. Here is the conjugation of the verb *to be* in its simplest form: present tense, indicative mood, active voice.

I **am**	we **are**
you **are**	you **are**
he, she, it **is**	they **are**

Here it is in the past tense:

I **was**	we **were**
you **were**	you **were**
he, she, it **was**	they **were**

To be is an **intransitive** verb, because it does not convey action to an object. Here are the same conjugations for a **transitive** verb, which can (although it does not have to) take an object.

I **buy**	we **buy**
you **buy**	you **buy**
he, she, it **buys**	they **buy**
I **bought**	we **bought**
you **bought**	you **bought**
he, she, it **bought**	they **bought**

In other languages verbs usually change their form as they change their person, but in English they usually don't change very much. Here, by contrast, are the present and past tenses of *amare*, the Latin infinitive for *to love*.

amo	amamus
amas	amatis
amat	amant
amabam	amabamus
amabas	amabatis
amabat	amabant

Imagine *lovabamus*. In this respect, at least, English is much easier than Latin and most other languages.

English has six basic tenses, categories carried over from Latin:

present: I write for a living. (The action is happening now.)

past (also called *perfect*): I *wrote* a story. (The action happened in the past, and is completed.)

imperfect: By that time I *was writing* in French. (The action happened in the past, but is perhaps not completed.)

past perfect: I *had written* that book before I decided to write this one. (The action was completed before another past action.)

future: I *will write* about that decision one of these days. (The action has not yet happened.)

future perfect: I *will have written* that story in time for the December issue. (The action has not yet happened, but the future in which it will happen is limited by some other event or condition.)

Notice that some of these forms use **auxiliary verbs** to complete their meaning. *To be* and *to have* are the most often used, but there are others—for example *to do* and *to go*. While more thoroughly inflected languages change the whole verb to express these variations, in English the change usually occurs only in the auxiliary verb. This limited inflection is another of the relatively few areas in which English is simpler than most other languages.

The use of auxiliary forms allows English verbs to express a great many aspects that a less flexible language like Latin would need adverbs to transmit. Here are some examples of the subtleties of action a verb form can express:

I *am writing* every day, but may not finish until June. (Continuous or progressive present action.)

I *have been writing* this story for some time now, but am growing tired of it. (Continuous or progressive past action.)

I *will be writing* this story for at least the next two years. (Continuous or progressive future action.)

By next August, I *will have been writing* this story for two years. (Continuous or progressive future perfect action.)

I *am going to* write that story one day. (Intention.)

I *was going to write* that story, but someone else did it first. (Past intention.)

I *do write* every day—please don't tell me I don't! (Emphasis.)

There are many more variations, and not every grammarian comes up with the same list. I am not trying (present progressive) to present a complete catalogue, but just to show that English auxiliary verbs are flexible instruments for communicating shades of meaning.

Verbs also have *moods* (see further discussion on pages 55–58.) All the above examples are in the **indicative mood**, which is the default form. The **subjunctive mood** is used for conditions doubted or contrary to fact, the **conditional mood** for referring to something that may happen only if something else happens first, and the **imperative mood** for commands. The conditional mood is sometimes referred to as merely a different tense, but it probably should not be blended in with the indicative tenses because, like the subjunctive, it hedges the likelihood of a statement's accuracy or truth.

I *will* never *write* again. (Future indicative.)

If I *were* rich (subjunctive, contrary to fact because I am not rich), I *would* never *write* again (future conditional, as it would only happen if something else in the future happened first).

Write the story by Friday! (Imperative.)

There used to be even more verb forms in English than there are today. Many have fallen into disuse, like those in these verses from Shakespeare's *Julius Caesar*, written around 1599.

If it were so, it *were* a grievous fault,
And grievously *hath* Caesar answered it.

Although most native speakers today would have trouble using these archaic forms correctly, few have any trouble understanding them.

ADJECTIVES (AND ARTICLES)

An *adjective* is a word that describes (or *modifies*) a noun or a pronoun.

Most adjectives are **qualitative adjectives**, because they describe the *quality* of the person, place, thing, or concept that they modify.

Music hath charms to soothe the *savage* breast.

Are those *nice* flowers for *little* me? What a *happy* thought!

Note that the word *savage* in the first example may be used as a noun as well as an adjective—which part of speech it is depends on how it is used in a sentence.

An adjective used as a noun is called a **substantive adjective**.

The *perfect* is the enemy of the *good*.

Two adjectives can be used together if they both modify the same noun.

Sarah uses the *old established* methods, allowing Christopher to practice those *new dangerous* ones.

Other adjectives are known as **limiting adjectives**, because they *limit* their nouns: how much? how many? which one?

There are at least *fourteen* ways of looking at that question; I will direct my attention to *several*.

Goldilocks turned toward the *largest* bear.

Proper adjectives are formed from proper nouns, and, like them, are capitalized.

I could eat one of those *Belgian* waffles.

Adjectives have **positive**, **comparative** and **superlative** forms.

hot, hotter, hottest

Some adjectives don't change their form, but add the words *more* or *most*.

beautiful, more beautiful, most beautiful

It is usually awkward (but not ungrammatical) to use *more* and *most* (or *less* and *least*) with an adjective that changes its form, but it is always incorrect to inflect one that does not change.

hot, more hot, most hot (odd and not favored, but in use)

beautiful, beautifuller, beautifullest (always to be avoided)

Some adjectives are irregular in their comparative and superlative forms

good, better, best

bad, worse, worst

There is, unfortunately, no absolute rule governing the choices available for the comparative forms of adjectives; you must learn them one at a time. Most native speakers have a sense that tells them when an adjective requires a particular comparative form. Often—but not always—it is the shorter adjectives that change.

Articles are generally treated as a subset of adjectives, not as a distinct part of speech (although some do think they are). English has three articles: *a, an,* and *the.*

The is called the **definite article** because it identifies a definite, particular individual. *A* and *an* are referred to as **indefinite articles** because they are more general.

That animal is a horse. (It could be any horse, but not a cow.)

That animal is the horse that won the Derby last year. (It could be only one horse.)

A is used before consonants, *an* before vowels to avoid slurred speech.

An artichoke, not **a** artichoke

A carrot, not **an** carrot

ADVERBS

Adverbs function like adjectives, but instead of describing or modifying a noun or a pronoun, an adverb describes or modifies a verb, an adjective, or another adverb.

He ate *slowly*. (*Slowly* modifies *ate*, a verb.)

The main course was *really* disgusting. (*Really* modifies *disgusting*, an adjective.)

It had been prepared *especially badly*. (*Badly* is an adverb modifying the verb *prepared*; *especially* is an adverb modifying the adverb *badly*.)

Comparison of adverbs is similar to that of adjectives. Many end in *-ly* and are regular; these require *more* or *most* (or *less* and *least*).

wickedly, more wickedly, most wickedly (never *wickedlier* or *wickedliest*)

Some are irregular.

well, better, best

And some, like *very* and *now*, do not ordinarily have comparative forms at all. As was the case with adjectives, there is no guide to forms of comparison but that derived from your own experience and intuition, matching the choices of informed speakers.

CONJUNCTIONS

Conjunctions, as the name suggests, join or connect other words or groups of words, whether single words, phrases, or clauses.

Coordinating conjunctions connect two or more elements of a sentence.

There is a remedy for everything, *but* not for death.

I will not laugh, *nor* will I cry.

She is a candidate without character *or* ideas.

The mnemonic acronym FANBOYS is sometimes used to recall the most common conjunctions: **f**or, **a**nd, **n**or, **b**ut, **o**r, **y**et, **s**o.

Correlative conjunctions work in pairs (or occasionally larger sets) to connect words with parallel functions in a sentence.

Both my wife *and* I thank you.

Not that I loved Caesar less, *but* that I loved Rome more.

Neither rain *nor* snow *nor* sleet *nor* gloom of night . . .

Coordinating and correlative conjunctions may also link verbs, adjectives, or adverbs.

Should we get something to eat *or* only to drink?

Hilda is tall, shy, *and* self-possessed.

She smiled bashfully *but* winningly.

Subordinating conjunctions act as a hinge between two clauses, one that can stand alone (an *independent clause*) and one that cannot (a *dependent clause*). Clauses are elements of a sentence which contain both a subject and a verb.

I won't speak to you *even if* you tear my hair out.

Subordinating conjunctions may initiate two or more consecutive clauses.

If you do not surrender, we will overpower you.

Although he was a crook and had spent time in jail, the people loved him.

Most subordinating conjunctions establish relations between the two clauses that are ***temporal*** (for example, *when* or *after*), ***causal*** (*for* or *because*), ***concessive*** (*although* or *even if*), or ***conditional*** (*unless* or *only if*).

Temporal
The dancers were sad *after* the ball was over.

He has been weeping *since* you left.

Causal
Since you could not be there, she invited someone else. (Note that *since* can be temporal or causal, according to context.)

He wandered around the city *because* he was feeling so lonely.

Concessive
I am so given to laughter, *even* your aunt Harriet cracks me up.

Although we cannot be there, we send you our love.

Conditional
Unless you stop singing immediately, I will leave.

I will stop singing *only if* you pay me.

Even if and *only if* are referred to as **compound conjunctions** because they are composed of more than one word.

PREPOSITIONS

Prepositions are words that clarify relations, often (but not always) of space (telling us where) or time (telling us when). They generally precede nouns or pronouns.

The bear went *over* the mountain.

It's always that way *with* me.

Oscar was *behind* the eight ball.

She was always *on* time.

The preposition and the noun which follows it (its **object**) combine to form a **prepositional phrase**.

The ball flew *over the outfielder's head* and bounced *to the wall*.

Love, let us be true *to one another*.

Prepositional phrases are used either like adjectives or like adverbs. The phrases just given extend the meaning of verbs or adjectives, and so are used as adverbs. The following extend the meaning of nouns or pronouns, and so are used as adjectives.

Portia has a degree *in chemical engineering*.

A body *at rest* tends to remain *at rest*.

Prepositions, alone or in combination with other prepositions, are often used as adverbs.

She was singing as they walked *along*.

They watched the kite sail *up above*.

For more on adverbial and adjectival prepositional phrases, see page 76.

INTERJECTIONS

The word **interjection** derives from the Latin *interiacere*, meaning *to throw between or among*. Interjections are so called because they are thrown in among other words without having a definite grammatical relation to them. They interrupt the flow of speech or writing to express a feeling like joy, anger, fear, or frustration.

Oh my goodness, I've locked the keys in the car again!

Dammit, Jerry, why don't you ever listen?

Interjections don't even have to be orthodox English words, but can be **onomatopoeic** (words which mimic sounds).

Eek, a ghost!

VERBALS

Verbals are special forms of verbs which don't behave like verbs. Instead they have the functions of nouns or adjectives. Even though they look exactly like verbs, they occupy a special category among the parts of speech.

English has three kinds of verbals: **participles**, which function as adjectives, and **gerunds** and **infinitives**, which function as nouns.

Participles describe a state of being in which the action of the verb is taking (or has taken) place.

The wound was *bleeding*.

Speaking as a doctor, I advise you not to smoke.

Standing there, he looked pathetic.

Despoiled of its leaves, the tree was bare.

On some occasions the present participle is not really acting as an adjective, but is part of a compound form of a verb, expressing a **progressive aspect** of the present tense.

Thus one could say, in the first of the examples given above, either that *bleeding* is an adjective modifying *wound* (that's the kind of wound it was) or that it is a verb, expressing the action of the wound (it bled and continued to bleed). This is of theoretical interest, but of little or no practical value.

Participles are either **present** or **past**.

Present participles end in *-ing* and describe a present condition. **Past participles** usually end in *-ed* and describe a past condition.

Lift not the *painted* veil which those who live call life. (Past participle.)

Our *concluding* thoughts were upbeat. (Present participle.)

Our revels now are *ended*. (Past participle.)

Some past participles are irregular and do not end in -ed.

The *written* word survives.

I like my steak well *done*.

Beware of the **dangling participle**, in which the element the participle modifies is missing or misplaced.

In America Henry found everyone confident but, *returning* to Europe, the mood was grave.

Grammatically this phrasing can only suggest that the

mood returned to Europe, while the obviously intended sense is that when *Henry* returned *he found* the mood there grave.

Having often *read* the Gettysburg Address, its words were echoed in her own.

The identity of the reader of Lincoln's words has been lost. The main clause should maintain the same subject as the one implied in the introductory phrase. Changing the main clause from passive to active, a good idea for stylistic reasons, solves this problem.

Having often *read* the Gettysburg Address, she echoed its words in her own.

Gerunds are verbal nouns, indistinguishable in form from present participles but different in function. Despite the fact that they share an *-ing* ending with participles, gerunds are always used as nouns. (The word *ending* in the previous sentence is an example.)

Parting is such sweet sorrow.

Running always tires me; I prefer *walking*.

I love *eating* pretzels.

It's not easy *being* green.

Infinitives are expressed in English by the word *to* and the simple form of the verb (sometimes called its **stem**).

To err is human.

Most cannot fail *to admire* her heroic behavior.

That's easy for you *to say*.

The word *to* in an infinitive is not a preposition or even a distinct part of speech, but a *particle*. It has no meaningful existence except when connected to its stem. It is part of a single unit, even if it is physically separated from its companion (for example, in a *split infinitive*). There is a vigorous controversy over the practice of splitting infinitives by putting another word between *to* and the stem. For more on this, see pages 51–55.

An infinitive, used as a noun, expresses the sense of the verb in more or less the same way as does a gerund.

Erring is human = *To err* is human.

I love *sleeping* late = I love *to sleep* late.

Saying that is easy = *To say* that is easy.

The **past infinitive** uses an auxiliary verb just as the past tense does.

It is better *to have loved* and *lost* than never *to have loved* at all.

Here *lost* is a part of the past infinitive *to have lost*, with the remaining words taken as understood.

It should once more be apparent that, in different contexts, some words may function as different parts of speech. For example, *knot* may be a noun or a verb (he tied a knot; you knot the rope); *fire* may be a noun, a verb, or even an adjective (the fire next door; you're fired; a fire truck). Their grammatical identity depends on their function.

PART II: THE SENTENCE

Now that you have a working sense of the parts of speech, the building blocks of grammatical discourse, we can consider the parts of the primary grammatical unit, the sentence, just as we might break a book into successively smaller units (parts, chapters, paragraphs, sentences, phrases, words, letters).

A **sentence** is traditionally described as *a complete thought*. For instance, a famous verse of the Bible (John 11:35) appears in many English versions as "Jesus wept" (on finding the family of Lazarus in mourning). No one has ever complained that this sentence needed development; it seems fully expressed exactly as it is.

Although no formal grammar of Aristotle's survives, he is remembered for discussing only two parts of speech, nouns and verbs. In doing so, he identified the major elements of the sentence: something (or someone) is doing something to something (or someone), or is having something done to it (or her or him), or is described as being in a certain state. It is generally true that everything else in a sentence modifies either the main noun or the main verb, whether directly or indirectly.

A sentence is the smallest *complete* set of words. Size has little to do with determining what makes up a sentence—only that it is a complete thought. As a result, single-word exclamations, commands, and responses to questions may stand alone as single thoughts and so be treated as complete sentences.

Wow!

Run!

Yes.

In speech (less often in formal writing), single-word clauses may be formed by leaving out terms that are understood.

"How old are you?" "[I am] *Thirty* [years old]."

The umpire shouted, "[The runner is] *Out!*"

These are exceptional cases. Ordinarily a sentence is made up of at least two words or logically related groups of words, one of which (a noun, a pronoun, or a verbal) is the **subject**, and the other (with a verb at its core) is the **predicate**. In the biblical text that appeared at the beginning of this section, *Jesus* is the subject and *wept* is the predicate.

Usually, but not always, a sentence also contains an **object**, which may be a **direct object** (receiving the action of the verb), an **indirect object** (receiving the direct object from the subject) or the **object of a preposition**.

You received my letter. (*You* is the pronoun subject; *letter* is the direct object.)

You sent my sister a letter. (*Letter* is the direct object, as it receives the action of sent; *sister* is the indirect object, because she received the object sent.)

You put the letter into your handbag. (The prepositional phrase *into your handbag* is part of the predicate of the sentence.)

Smiling the whole time, you put the letter into your handbag. (The phrase *smiling the whole time* refers to the subject *you* and thus is part of the subject of the sentence.)

You put the letter into your handbag, smiling the whole time. (*Smiling the whole time* is still part of the subject even though it comes at the end of the sentence. It is the *function* of the words, not their order in a sentence, that determines their grammatical identity.)

Note: In some cases the context determines function. In the last example, just above, *smiling the whole time* is understood to refer to *you*. But if the sentence were to read *You put the letter into your handbag there beside you on the chair*, it would be clear that the phrase referred to the handbag.

A group of words with a subject and a predicate operates as an independent grammatical unit. It can be a sentence on its own (like *Jesus wept*), or it can be part of a larger sentence, in which case it is called a **clause**. If the clause can stand by itself as a complete sentence, it is an **independent clause**; if not, it is a **dependent clause**.

Henry shouted and nobody noticed. (Two independent clauses—*nobody noticed* could stand alone as a sentence.)

I knew he was crying because I saw his tears. (An independent clause followed by a dependent one—*because I saw his tears* cannot stand alone.)

A group of words having *neither* a subject *nor* a predicate is a **phrase** rather than a clause.

Sarah was silent, *calming her associates*.

Dressed all in white, she seemed serene.

We can classify sentences as **simple**, **compound**, **complex** and **compound-complex**.

Henry moped all that morning, right through lunch, continuing without a break until sunset. (This is a simple sentence despite its many phrases, because there is only one verb and so only one predicate, and therefore only one clause.)

Henry moped and then he felt better. (This is a compound sentence, composed of two independent clauses.)

Henry moped because everything was just too much for him. (This is a complex sentence. It starts with an independent clause. Then *because* begins a dependent clause with a subject [*everything*] and a predicate [*was just too much for him*]. Since this part of the sentence cannot stand alone, it is a dependent clause. Having two different types of clauses makes the sentence complex.)

Henry moped because everything was just too much and because he didn't want to suffer anymore. (This sentence is compound-complex because it has three clauses and at least one of them is dependent on one of the other two.)

Usually (although not always) a sentence without a subject and a predicate is not a sentence at all but a **sentence fragment**:

Henry moping all day long. (Where is the verb? *Moping* is a participle and thus acts as an adjective, not as a verb. "Henry *was moping*." is a complete sentence.)

All through the day, and the night too, and the next day, moping as though his heart would break, refusing all consolation. (Where's the subject? Where's the main verb? The clause "as though his heart would break" is dependent, but there is no main clause for it to depend on.)

Sentence fragments are common in speech, but are disfavored in formal writing except in poems, or as a deliberate gesture toward informality.

SEE EXERCISE 1: Kinds of Clauses, page 87.

PART III: SOME PRACTICAL CONSIDERATIONS BRIDGING GRAMMAR AND USAGE

In his *Ars Major*, Donatus discussed two broad kinds of errors, **barbarism** and **solecism**. *Barbarism* indicated a mispronunciation (or misspelling) of a single word, while *solecism* referred to errors like failure of agreement between verb and noun, or of number between noun and adjective. In other words, solecisms force the language to do what its rules specifically forbid. Since many of Donatus' examples are drawn from the text of Virgil's *Aeneid*, solecism cannot be all bad. Virgil was Rome's greatest poet, and so his linguistic misbehavior was almost certainly intentional, reflecting *poetic license*. Without poetic license, solecisms translate into what we would call *grammatical errors*. We ourselves may feel licensed to break the rules and, as long as we do so convincingly and with knowledge, we can usually persuade our reader or listener that we are behaving reasonably. If so, not only will we be able to get away with a solecism, we may even be admired for it; those who really understand the rules may break them with impunity. This section is mainly concerned with various kinds of solecism.

Agreement: person, number, case, and gender

Failure to preserve grammatical agreement is perhaps the main source of misspeaking and faulty writing in English. The word *agreement* is used here in a technical sense: *All* related grammatical elements in a sentence *must* agree with one another.

A verb must agree with its subject (agreement of person).

I think, therefore I am.
not
I think, therefore I is.

There are occasional anomalies even with this simplest of rules.

William and Mary are friends.
but
William & Mary is a college.

An adjective must agree in number with the noun it modifies.

A person should keep his [*or* her *or* his or her] options open.
not
A person should keep their options open.

A noun and a pronoun must reflect each other's gender.

All my men are out on *their* patrols.
not
All my men are out on *his or her* patrols.
and not
Each of my men is out on *his or her* patrol.

Pronouns must reflect their case.

The teacher *whom* I like
not
The teacher *who* I like

Latin had a highly developed system of cases with specially inflected endings. Every noun, pronoun, and adjective had five major cases (*nominative, genitive, dative, accusative,* and *ablative*) as well as two minor ones (*vocative* and *locative*). Although the English system is simpler, it has cases, too— the **subjective, possessive,** and **objective.**

The **subjective case** (corresponding to the Latin *nominative*) is used for the subject of a sentence or a clause, or for a word standing grammatically in the subject's place, even if that word appears in the predicate of the sentence.

Bob, my uncle, is a teacher.

Bob, uncle and *teacher* are all in the subjective case and all describe the same person. The word *uncle* is in **apposition** to *Bob,* as both are in the subject's part of the sentence; *teacher* is a **predicate noun.**

The **possessive case** denotes a relationship in which one entity belongs to another.

The taste of *Dan's* sandwich reminded Esther of her *mother's* cooking.

The sandwich is Dan's, but the cooking is that of Esther's mother.

The **objective case** (corresponding to the Latin *accusative*) refers to the object of a verb in a clause.

Dan ate his *sandwich*.

Sandwich is a **direct object**, because it receives the action of the verb *ate*.

Other relations, which take other cases in Latin, also require the use of the objective in English. For example an **indirect object**, which takes the *dative* case in Latin, may be expressed in English without a preposition to signal its case.

Dan gave the *dog* his sandwich.

The word *dog* is not the direct object of the sentence (receiving the action of the verb), *sandwich* is. Since the action of the verb passes directly to the sandwich and then indirectly on to the dog, the dog is the indirect object. But it is still an object, and so it takes the objective case.

An indirect object often has a pronoun in front of it, which can be omitted and only implied. The pronoun is usually *to*, but it could be another, such as *for* or *at*. This sentence could also be written as follows:

Dan gave his sandwich *to the dog*.

That last element we normally (and correctly) identify as a prepositional phrase. Here, however, it also expresses the indirect object of the verb.

The rule is that grammatically related words need to agree with one another in either a singular or a plural form. This is a simple rule and should ordinarily cause no difficulty. A problem arises, however, with ***collective nouns***, that is, singular nouns representing a group. We have options with them and can treat them as seems most logical in a given context.

Although the *crowd* in the Colosseum *was calling* for blood, at least *several* in it *were rooting* for the Christians.

Treating the subject of the first clause, *crowd*, as plural might create confusion in the main clause, with its plural subject *several* and plural verb *were rooting*. (Note that using the singular *was* for *crowd* forces the use of the singular pronoun *it*.)

Although the *crowd* in the Colosseum *were calling* for blood, at least several among them were rooting for the Christians.

Note that British practice is sometimes different from American—the British are more likely to treat an organization (which is actually a group of people) as plural.

Standard Oil Company of Ohio *has changed its* policy.

British Petroleum Company *have changed their* policy.

The second example sounds wrong to American ears, but it is the result of a different convention. In America a corporation is singular even if its name is in a plural form.

American Airlines *has changed its* policy.

Airlines is part of the name of the company and therefore a proper noun. However, changed to lowercase, *airlines* becomes a common noun and takes its normal plural number.

All American airlines *have changed their* policy.

The grammatical need for subjects and verbs to agree in number can force us to some ungainly expressions.

Some of the *knives look* like *they* need sharpening, but *none looks* as though *it* should be thrown away.

Some, a limiting adjective, is plural because the word *knives* is plural and requires the plural verb *look* and the plural pronoun *they*. But *none* is singular, understood as *no one* (singular because *one* is singular), and so requires the singular verb *looks* and the singular pronoun *it*. Some grammarians would dispute this judgment. John Beall, for instance, offers the following observation, which we may study as a model sentence:

> *None* of you grammarians *are going* to persuade me that "none" is always singular.

While one is sympathetic to Beall's pragmatic sense of the implied plurality of *none* on some (even on most) occasions, *none* still means *no one*. For some reason most of us sense the expressly singular status of such related words as *nobody* and *anybody*, but for *none* we tend to tolerate plurality:

> None dare call it treason.

Nonetheless, in response to Beall, it seems at least possible (and surely reasonable) to offer the following rebuttal, also in the form of a model sentence:

> *None* of you contrarian grammarians *is going* to persuade me that Beall is right.

In fact, Beall's rejoinder offers an excellent example of the need to choose among two essentially correct (or at least not incorrect) formulations, knowing that, whatever choice we make, we will offend someone while pleasing someone else. The essential point is that we enjoy considerable leeway in our linguistic choices *if* we make them consciously and are capable of defending them.

Perhaps nothing in the fetid grammatical atmosphere we are all breathing is more disturbing than the frequent presence of the so-called **singular they**. This usage should be seen as plain error, but is tolerated by some, perhaps to avoid the stilted, awkward *he or she* construction.

As an example, consider the following sentence:

If a *writer* does not wish to offend the female reader, *they* should avoid male-gendered general pronouns.

I confess it hurt to compose that sentence even as an example of what should never be uttered or written. Nonetheless, this ungrammatical practice has been gaining unofficial and official *cachet* in the past forty years—indeed it has a long history as a not-very-often-used alternative even in a few passages in Shakespeare and other British and American classics, when grammatical rules were looser than they became in the eighteenth century.

For a brief and clear review of this problem and a list of potential solutions, see the section on gender-neutral pronouns on Michael Quinion's *World Wide Words* web-site, *http://www. worldwidewords.org/articles/genpr.htm*. I agree with Quinion that no single solution seems likely to win general—much less universal—assent. Avoidance may be the best solution. For instance, we might recast that offensive example as follows:

If *writers* do not wish to offend the general reader, *they* should avoid use of "singular they."

As the Italians say, *c'è sempre una terza via* (there's always another way). Thus I deplore Quinion's willingness to deploy a solecism if he can thereby "avoid sexism."

Just this last year, asked to write a recommendation for a student who wanted to enroll in a graduate program, I found myself reading the following from an admissions officer at one of the senior and most respected universities in this country.

Has the student mastered the required background information for graduate school? **Do they have** the maturity and motivation to succeed? How well **do they express themselves** in speech and writing? Please estimate **the applicant's** potential.

I did not send that university my opinion of its official English, and (possibly as a result) the student was admitted. Another university administrator recently told a reporter:

"If **the student** is at this level of qualification, it's likely that **they'll** be admitted."

Sensitivity to potential offense has caused a large amount of compositional strangeness. As long ago as 1994, the lawyer for rap star Tupac Shakur apparently described a proposed evidentiary order in his client's case as "asking me to trust the **fox** when **he or she** is entering the chicken coop." We all should avoid the sloppiness of that administrator and the hyper-correctness of that lawyer.

The morning I started work on this book, I heard a news broadcast about the Wimbledon tennis championship. The announcer, speaking about two American players whose matches were delayed by rain, said: "It seems unlikely that **either guy** will complete **their** contest today." Here we see grammar uselessly sacrificed to imagined gender-correctness—uselessly because the players were both male.

Each side in this debate may have a political interest. The grammarian in us needs to be aware of that, but should also maintain allegiance to the urgent and apolitical claims of linguistic clarity. George Orwell is only one of the twentieth-century writers who warned us of the other erosions that follow the wearing away of clear speech. Gender-correct but grammatically disastrous speech should not be an acceptable alternative to anyone of taste and judgment.

Writers and speakers of English need to face up to this challenge. In the good old days speakers and writers understood that the masculine (*he, him, himself, his*) was universal. It indicated *either* a specifically male referent *or* a being not identified by gender, who might be male or female. The textbook's rubric for this situation held that *the masculine includes the feminine*. This was an economical and sensible way of dealing with an ambiguity inherent in English usage. Whatever its usefulness, it is now generally unwelcome.

Somewhere along the way we speakers of English should have invented a gender-neutral pronoun that referred to animate subjects (otherwise *it* would have served), for instance, *hef*. We then would be able to choose among *he, she, hef,* and *it.* The passages from the university's questionnaire (referred to above) could then have read:

> Does **hef** have the maturity and motivation to succeed? How well does **hef** express **hefself** in speech and writing?

Some writers have tried to fill the hef-gap with *s/he* and *hir*, which have the virtue of sounding and reading like grammatically correct female-inclusive pronouns. These are perhaps better than *hef*, but I admit I do not enjoy using them, or other forms of inoffensiveness I happen to find offensive, including the table-turning use of *she* as the all-gender-embracing pronoun—on the principle, one supposes, that "You had your turn for five hundred years, now it's ours."

When I have to compose a similar passage, whether in speech or in writing, I sometimes compromise my sense of pleasing English style to the politics of gendered grammar and resort to *he or she.* I try, nonetheless, to avoid these constructions. It's all a matter of taste and choice. "Do what you will" is the whole of the law here, but you must will consistently, be prepared to live with the result, and be aware that, if you buy into the rule-bending and common-sense-assaulting excesses of gender-correct ways of speaking and writing, some of us out here will think less of you. There is a person, now president of a college, who one summer some years ago cleaned out offendingly gendered vocabulary from a major university's official publications. Hef decided the word *manual* was a male-hegemonic term and replaced it with *handbook* (I am not making this up). Hef apparently did not know that *manual* derives from the Latin word *manus*, meaning *hand* (a noun of the fourth declension that just happens to have the feminine gender). I still smile at the memory of such misplaced zeal.

Three years ago we acquired a German Shepherd puppy. I read two dog manuals, and found no *s/he*, no *him-or-her*, as I would have found in handbooks about babies. Every puppy was *he*. What a relief! Even though our beloved Josie is female, I had no problem linking the instructions to her needs. That experience made clear just how much usage has been changed by cultural sensitivities. Canine gender-correctness has not yet overtaken us.

See EXERCISE 2: Agreement, page 88.

SPLIT INFINITIVES

May we split infinitives? Should we? That is, should we put another word between *to* and the verb stem?

To know her is *to really love* her.

If we have a choice (and we always do), we probably would not want to split an infinitive. Most of us simply do not realize that in fact we have a choice. I do not think I ever have split an infinitive, at least not in writing, as permissive on this issue as even some prescriptive grammarians have become.

Here again we cross the line between *grammar* and *usage*. The generally acknowledged master of this subject is Henry Watson Fowler (1858–1933), whose *Dictionary of Modern English Usage*, first published in England in 1926, is the favored scripture of grammatical purists. In his view,

> **The English-speaking world may be divided into (1) those who neither know nor care what a split infinitive is; (2) those who do not know, but care very much; (3) those who know and condemn; (4) those who know and approve; and (5) those who know and distinguish.**

Fowler is surely right that there is no *law* to keep us from splitting infinitives. Nonetheless not splitting them is a centuries-old *habit*, based on a sense that *to* and a verb stem form an indivisibly meaningful unit, even if (unlike a Latin or French or Spanish infinitive), it is expressed by more than a single word. There are only three possibilities: adverbs modifying infinitives may precede, split, or follow them. As Fowler says, "It is of no avail merely to fling oneself desperately out of temptation"—one must choose.

Fowler's choice of the awkward *merely to fling* shows that even while arguing for relative permissiveness, he preferred to avoid a split. Indeed, most of the examples he gives of unsplit infinitives seem fussy or maladroit. But if not fussy, a split infinitive need not be maladroit. Take this example from Fowler, followed by two variations.

intended to better equip successful candidates for careers in India

intended better to equip successful candidates for careers in India

intended to equip successful candidates better for careers in India

All three are acceptable, but not equally satisfying. *To better equip* sounds natural, but the split offends purists. *Better to equip* avoids a split at the cost of fussiness. *To equip ... better* expresses the same idea clearly and unfussily, offends no one, and avoids a cumbersome recasting such as *to equip successful candidates ... with better skills*. Putting the adverb after the infinitive is often the cleanest and best solution.

If you want to use an infinitive with a modifying adverb, you will need to make a decision about what seems most effective and euphonious.

Let's work together to completely conquer this problem.

That is relatively inoffensive as split infinitives go. Is *completely to conquer* an improvement? It sounds forced and over-correct. What about *to conquer this problem completely*? Better, I think. Here again, moving the adverb to the end of the clause is both more logical and more natural-sounding.

Recasting the sentence is certainly an attractively flexible alternative. How does *Let's work together to eradicate this problem* sound? Or *Let's solve this problem once and for all by working together*? As is so often the case, a problem can defeat us if we have only a narrow sense of its potential solution.

On his website at *http://alt-usage-english.org*, Mark Israel expresses the view of many students of the problem:

> **Hardly any serious commentator believes that infinitives should never be split. The dispute is between those who believe that split infinitives should be avoided when this can be done with no sacrifice of clarity or naturalness, and those who believe that no effort whatever should be made to avoid them.**

While close to agreement with Mr. Israel, I would like to play a little game with him. Suppose, instead of saying *infinitives should never be split*, he had written *infinitives are never to be split*. Would he have then been equally comfortable with *infinitives are to never be split*? I doubt it—I certainly would not. And so good practice is to avoid splitting infinitives unless you cannot find another way to express yourself precisely—an unlikely eventuality. And I will give you a dollar for every split infinitive you can convince me really *needed* to be split, if you will give me a penny for each one I can save you from splitting. If we both had a lot of free time, I would end up rich.

I want you to all really do your best.

That is not a sentence I could ever approve. *All* is clearly not part of the infinitive, and so my revision might run:

I want you all to really do your best.

Look what I have just done! By mending the more egregious sin (*all* sounds really ugly after *to*), I have allowed myself to split *to* and *do*. Must I? Isn't *really to do* better here? Or is there, once again, another and still better way? As is often the case in English, intensifying adverbs like *really*, *truly*, and *surely* often weaken a claim by making it seem self-serving. Like the Player Queen, in the view of Hamlet's mother, they protest too much.

I want you all to do your best.

I think that is a clear improvement, achieved by omitting an unnecessary adverb.

Here, perhaps trying for a record, is a spokesperson for presidential candidate Barack Obama, quoted in the *Wall Street Journal* in 2008:

Despite the best efforts of the Clinton campaign *to once again cynically diminish* the caucus process …

A triple split infinitive! Poor Hillary never had a chance.

The Subjunctive Mood

English verbs have at least nine moods, representing various levels of likelihood or reality. The four most important of these are the **indicative**, **imperative**, **subjunctive**, and **conditional**. The indicative mood, used for statements of things generally accepted to be true, gives little difficulty; neither does the imperative mood, used for commands. But the subjunctive mood (often operating alongside the conditional) does sometimes cause confusion.

Just as *whom* is giving place to *who* (see page 62), even when its grammatical role clearly calls for the objective case, so common usage is replacing subjunctive forms with indicative ones. Not many people still use all the available subjunctive forms, and among those who do, many say them either automatically or by imitating phrases heard or read, without knowing exactly why.

The subjunctive mood is often found in the verb of a subordinate clause where the main clause is in the conditional mood, expressing a condition or a circumstance not existing at present, but feared, longed for, or imagined in place of what is.

If I *were* president, I *would ban* singing in the streets.

Had I *been* president, I *would have banned* singing in the streets.

If you *had* the time, I *would explain* all this more clearly.

Had you *had* the time, I *would have explained* all this more clearly.

In the first sentence, the speaker acknowledges not being president, and so the intention to ban singing is only conditional. Only if this condition *were* realized would the speaker try to do this ("Now that I am president, I will ban singing"). This form of the subjunctive is still common.

Compare two nearly identical sentences, the first in the indicative, dealing with events that have actually occured, the second dealing with a condition that did not occur, leaving the conditional action incomplete.

Since I knew you were coming, I prepared the spare bed.

Had I *known* you were coming, I *would have prepared* the spare bed.

Use of the subjunctive denotes questionable or uncertain conditions in past and even in future tenses, with the help of auxiliary elements such as *let, may, might* and *should*. The key question is always whether a condition that is either *uncertain*, or *contrary to present fact*, colors the meaning of the verb.

Let there *be* light. (And there was light, which there hadn't been before.)

May I *be struck* dead if I lie. (But not if I don't.)

Might she not *have asked* for mercy? (She might have, but she did not.)

The subjunctive mood is perhaps the most sophisticated matter touched on in this introduction to English grammar. Fortunately the requirement for its use is such that most of us rarely need to deploy it in our daily lives; at the same time, it is important to be able to recognize it when it leaps out at you from behind a tree on a dark and stormy night.

See EXERCISE 3: The Subjunctive, page 88.

LEVELS OF DISCOURSE

It is customary to distinguish between *formal speech* (usually thought of as written, but sometimes read aloud, a depressing habit of many public speakers in this country) and *informal speech* (generally thought of as spoken, although e-mails and tweets are closer to it than letters are). There is a certain merit in that simple distinction. However, some spoken English is very formal indeed, while some written language is very informal. The important thing to remember is that any utterance, whether written or spoken, is the product of choice. The speaker or writer is often trying to align hefself with (or, in some instances, against) a particular audience. "Friends, Romans, countrymen, lend me your ears" in Shakespeare's *Julius Caesar* is a call for attention aimed toward a crowd by someone who wants to sway it (or them). "Now listen up, youse guys" might show a similar intent, but in a very different stylistic register. Which style to choose will vary with a speaker's intent and sense of the audience.

Milan Kundera, exploring the manipulative nature of

political rhetoric in his novel *The Joke* (1967), portrays a Czech bureaucrat making a speech that began in sentimentality and then progressed to unvarnished political harangue.

> He spoke of spring, of flowers, of mamas and papas, he also spoke of love, which according to him bore fruit, but suddenly his vocabulary was transformed and the words duty, responsibility, the State, and citizen appeared; suddenly there was no more papa and mama, but father and mother. . . .

When you are setting out to write or to say something, you need to decide what effect you are trying to attain. For instance, you might attempt to convince, commiserate with, condemn, or congratulate the reader or hearer of your words; at times a combination of aims will motivate you. What implications do these choices have for your grammatical decisions? Are there situations in which you might deliberately trash "good grammar"?

> If you expect me to say terrible things about her, then I ain't your boy.

> If you expect me to say terrible things about her, then you might wish to approach someone else instead.

The first example probably establishes the unalterable firmness of your position better than more "correct" phrasing has the power to do. On the other hand, there are some people you would probably *not* want to address in the "low style." Once again, it is a matter of strategy and taste. The most important thing about your expressive life is that it is *yours*. You enjoy the right to choose the language you present yourself in. Almost anything is allowable, *as long as you convince your audience that you know what you are doing*. And in order to have that effect in writing (and to some degree in speaking), you must first develop an awareness of grammar, which underlies all human discourse. In a grammarless world, we might have to gesticulate or grunt in order to make clear the relations among our words. Language is the grammatical arrangement of words; without grammar, we have only vocabulary, not language.

You knock on a friend's door. From behind it comes "Who's there?" You reply, "It's me." Should you have said "It is I"? That is more grammatically correct, since a subjective case is clearly called for where a predicate pronoun follows a verb of being. But how many people actually speak "correctly" in this situation? I expect there are not many.

Two considerations are at work here. Bad grammar is sometimes good usage, while good grammar is sometimes an offensive example of self-conscious hyper-correctness, and thus bad usage. Purists may insist that we must always say *It is I* because the first-person pronoun is in the subjective case. But hardly anyone does so, even in fairly formal discourse—here the language has simply outgrown Latin grammar. (Some might argue that *It's me* follows correct French practice [*c'est moi*, and not *c'est je*].)

Well, should you say *It is I*? Sometimes this works well—thus the King James Bible has Jesus say "It is I; be not afraid" (Matthew 14:27). But today, use *it is I* only if you feel like it, only if you want your listeners or readers to consider you super-refined and over-educated. There may be times when you want to do exactly that. But when the bartender in the local bar on a busy Saturday night looks through the crowd and wants to know who is the guy who just asked for the two English ales, I don't think you'd want to say anything else but *It's me* (or maybe just *Yo!*). And I'd leave off "and lest you think I have just committed a solecism, my good man, I want you to know that I have employed the French disjunctive pronoun." Pow, right in the kisser!

In this discussion we have reached the nearly invisible line that separates *usage* from *style*. *Usage* has to do with what most expert practitioners consider correct speech or writing, *style* with what they consider effective use of language. However, everyone ought to know, and even to insist, that there is little certainty in separating acceptable from unacceptable usage, or pleasing from unpleasant style.

In E. B. White's words (from his revised version of *The Elements of Style*),

> There is no satisfactory explanation of style, no infallible guide to good writing, no assurance that a person who thinks clearly will be able to write clearly, no key that unlocks the door, no inflexible rule by which the young writer may shape his course.

In this balanced, five-part rhetorical flourish, White convinces us of two things: that the path to effective style is a hidden one and that, if we imitate him wisely, we may have some hope of finding it. The section that follows examines problems encountered in ordinary speech nearly every day; it offers clear ways of dealing with them by the application of simple rules.

(1) WHO OR WHOM?

It is pretty clear that making a decision to adapt a rule to a chosen level of discourse may require sacrifice, weighing our loyalty to orthodoxy against our sense of current vernacular practice. For instance, the choice between *who* and *whom* is treated variously in current discussions about speech and even about writing. This **relative pronoun** (relating the phrase or clause that follows to a preceding noun) is *who* in the subjective case (as the subject of the clause it introduces). It is *whose* in the possessive case; in the objective case, either as the direct or indirect object of a verb or as the object of a preposition, it is *whom*. Similarly, when used as an interrogative pronoun, *who* is subjective, while *whom* is objective. In theory, whenever the pronoun *who*, whether relative or interrogative, is preceded by any preposition or is used as an object of a verb or preposition, we should use *whom*.

Send not to know **for whom** the bell tolls.

Whom did you say you had offended?

Whose pencil did she borrow?

The problematic nature of the choice arises from the fact that these rules are slowly changing, as rules do in a living language, and *whom* is fading from current use, especially in speech.

Gwendolyn, **to whom** I lent my etchings, left town with them.

Bill Mazeroski, **whom** Zazie will never forgive, hit that home run.

"**Whom** do you think you're talking to?" shouted Buzz.

These three sentences move along a scale from formal to more informal diction. I think it is fair to say that the first phrasing represents something like common consent. Few would say or write *to who I lent my etchings*. On the other hand, changing the sentence only slightly, we find that separating the preposition from its object permits a greater latitude. A relative clause like *who I lent my etchings to* may be unorthodox, but is certainly in widespread use. Although formally incorrect, it has vernacular currency—that is, a person who would not be caught dead saying it still has to admit that he or she understands its meaning without difficulty, and might hefself slip unconsciously into such expression in speaking. This is much less likely to happen when the preposition directly precedes the pronoun.

With regard to the second example, my guess is that about half of those writing it and most of those saying it would not honor the grammatical force of the objective case: *who Zazie will never forgive* is thus wrong grammatically but alive and strong.

As for the third sentence, even I must admit that hardly any living American would follow that practice in speech—or in writing. *Who do you think you're talking to?* is simply more accurate as a way of recording an angry person's way of speaking—or indeed a placid one's. Nonetheless, old fogey that I am, I would still say (and surely write) *whom*. And I will admire you if you do, too.

The late Peter Gomes of the Harvard Divinity School gave the commencement address at Collegiate School in New York City in 2002. It was the best commencement address I ever heard. "The three short things for you to remember in life are these," he said.

1. It is not *who* you know in life, it's *whom*.
2. It's the second mouse that gets the cheese.
3. Good judgment comes from experience, and experience comes from bad judgment.

That first observation received general approbation and a one-man standing ovation. But what if Gomes, a champion of grammatical correctness, had been at a recent graduation ceremony at a university that considers itself in Harvard's class and heard the valedictorian say:

> The environment at this university encourages you to focus intensely on your interests, under the

guidance of people *who* you would otherwise read *about*.

That valedictorian would probably never allow himself to say *about who*. Because he had grown sloppy (and perhaps had been encouraged in this by our current academic culture, which does not make grammar a priority), separating the preposition from its object caused him to embarrass himself in front of all who observe the rules. How important is that? Perhaps not so very important to most people. In fact, few educated people would *deliberately* speak this way. If you feel comfortable demonstrating ignorance, by all means continue to do so. You will have lots of company. On the other hand, there will be people like me lining the avenue when you march by. We will be feeling sorry for you.

(2) *LIKE* OR *AS*?

Problems of usage often have their roots in misapplied grammatical principles. One consequence of a developed sense of grammar is that you will find yourself surprised by the linguistic behavior even of learned writers and speakers. A common cause of confusion is the choice between *like* and *as*. *Like* is almost always used as a preposition, taking a noun or pronoun as its object.

Kerouac didn't look *like* your usual man of letters.

By contrast, *as* usually indicates action.

He moved *as* does a man who is armed and dangerous.

Usually, but not always:

Like a mighty army moves the Church of God.

His strength was *as* the strength of ten, because his heart was pure.

SEE EXERCISE 4: *like or as?*, page 89.

(3) BETWEEN OR AMONG?

Still another prepositional confusion comes with *between* and *among*. *Between* is used for pairs; *among* for three or more.

I saw Benedict seated *between* Francis and Augustine, while Gabriel was flying *among* the myriad angels.

He whispered, "Just *between* the two of us, I never cared for theological treatises."

At that, *among* the theologians, one was aware of a resentful shudder.

Tonight, you find yourself *among* your many friends.

Tonight, you find yourself *between* your only two friends.

It has become fashionable, in some grammatical circles,

to deride those who insist on maintaining this distinction, even though the origins of both words point clearly to its validity. According to the *Shorter Oxford English Dictionary*, *between* descends from ancient English, Saxon, and German words all of which indicate or imply "twoness," while *among* derives from Old English *mong*, referring to a "crowd." The dictionary continues by offering examples. Among (not between) others (there are more than two), Katherine Mansfield is cited as follows: "She looked fascinating in her black suit, something *between* a bishop and a fly." And we are offered the words of Daphne du Maurier: "If I heard it, even *among* a thousand others, I should recognise her voice." It seems clear that substitution of either word for the other in those two sentences would not be a good idea. Since you cannot be ruled wrong if you honor this distinction, simple to learn and easy to keep, it is probably advisable to do so.

SEE EXERCISE 5: *between* or *among*?, page 90.

(4) *DUE TO* OR *BECAUSE OF*?

When should we use *due to*, and when *because of*?

Today's game was postponed **due to** rain.

Today's game was postponed **because of** rain.

I prefer the second solution, because *due to* ordinarily introduces an adjectival phrase, and *because of* introduces an adverbial phrase. The intent to modify the verb *was postponed* calls for an adverbial phrase, and so *because of* is preferred. *Due to*, like *owing to*, introduces an adjectival phrase, and so should be used in preference to *because of*. If you are content to follow common practice, this distinction is not important, but for clarity and persuasive power "correct" grammar is often best. Choosing the soundest option in grammatical terms will probably offend no one, and may give your voice a satisfying and effective tone of authority.

When I was a boy, this argument was confined to the first two of these phrases. Then someone raised the possibility that *owing to* might substitute for *due to*. I confess I never saw the reasoning behind this maneuver. Nonetheless, there are widely divergent views about whether there is any discernible difference among the grammatical values of *due to*, *because of*, and *owing to*. There is some intelligent support for each of the following positions:

(1) All three have the same grammatical value; therefore they may be used interchangeably.

(2) *Due to* is adjectival and *because of* adverbial, while *owing to* may be used either way.

(3) Both *due to* and *owing to* are adjectival, while *because of* is adverbial.

The third choice represents my position. Am I right? Most "experts" would say that I am not, but that I am old-fashioned (true enough) and a stickler for outmoded rules (less true). Let me ask these critics if anything I have urged you to do is *wrong*. They will have to admit that at least *some* people *do* observe these distinctions, and thus could consider careless use of these phrases *wrong*, but no one could take exception to saying it the other way. What can you lose if you follow the stricter rule?

SEE EXERCISE 6: *due to* or *because of?*, page 90

(5) WHICH OR THAT?

This distinction, once observed by nearly all who had been even slightly educated, has largely been erased from the minds even of those who ought to know it. Both these relative pronouns are used to introduce adjectival clauses describing or modifying substantives (nouns, like *women,* or nominal phrases, like *the Princeton University women's championship tennis team*). Is there a rule governing which of these two relative pronouns to use? Yes. *That* introduces restrictive clauses; *which* introduces nonrestrictive clauses. Restrictive clauses modify or describe nouns by adding *defining or necessary* details, while nonrestrictive clauses add information that, while perhaps of interest, is *not necessary* for identification. (To recall which kind of clause takes which pronoun, remember *that* and *restrictive* are the shorter words, *which* and *nonrestrictive* are the longer.)

The pen *that* rested in the inkwell reminded me of a bird.

The pen, *which* rested in the inkwell, reminded me of a bird.

In the first sentence, a particular pen, distinct from any other, is singled out by the use of a restrictive clause from among all other pens, visible or not. In the second sentence, the nonrestrictive clause simply adds additional non-essential information about this particular pen, an object already known and recognized.

The article *that* you sent me was of special interest.

The article, *which* you sent me, was of special interest.

The typewriter *that* used to be on my desk has been replaced by a computer.

The typewriter, *which* used to be on my desk, has been replaced by a computer.

The mahogany chest *that* Phoebe loves is still right where grandmother left it.

The mahogany chest, *which* Phoebe loves, is still right where grandmother left it.

In the first sentence in all three pairs, the relative clause contains information which separates the thing it describes from all others, thus "restricting" the range of meaning of the noun it modifies. In the second sentences, the clause is not restrictive.

In the first sentence of the final pair, the fact that Phoebe loves the chest is presented as its defining characteristic—the other chests, which she did not love, have been moved since grandmother's day. In the second, the parenthetical nature of this additional information is reflected by the commas that separate it from the rest of the sentence.

Nonrestrictive *which* clauses are set off by commas; restrictive *that* clauses are not. Perhaps if we found parentheses setting off nonrestrictive clauses rather than commas we would have an easier time recognizing them (and composing them). Unfortunately, grammar, like life, is not fair.

(6) DANGLING PREPOSITIONS

There used to be a "rule" which demanded with urgency and firmness that no one should ever end a sentence with a preposition. This rule may be traced to the grammarian Bishop Robert Lowth, who laid it down in his *Short Introduction of English Grammar* (1762). Lowth said:

> This is an Idiom which our language is strongly inclined to[!]; it prevails in common conversation, and suits very well with the familiar style in writing; but the placing of the Preposition before the Relative is more graceful, as well as more perspicuous; and agrees much better with the solemn and elevated Style.

Lowth's reasoning was based on aesthetics and rhetoric, not on grammar, and the time has surely come to let common sense overcome this daffy prohibition, which he himself broke even as he presented it.

I would answer the door, but I have nothing *on*.

That preposition certainly dangles, but the sentence is grammatically sound.

(7) Nouns used as adjectives

Speaking of adjectives, we should usually avoid using nouns as their equivalents, a lazy habit that has become increasingly common. To be fair, some such usage has become so ingrained that there seems no way to avoid it: *baseball glove, Kenyon students, dairy farmer, practice field, potato pancakes*. Ways of avoiding these familiar phrases and others like them seem clumsy and artificial (*glove for catching baseballs, students attending Kenyon College, farmer who keeps cows for their milk, field for practicing, pancakes made from potatoes*).

Nonetheless, phrases like *mathematics ability, grammar expertise, instruction manual,* and *sex appetite* are at least potentially offensive to some hearers, who might respond in a friendlier way to *mathematical ability, grammatical expertise, instructional manual,* and *sexual appetite*. Unfortunately, this is not an area that can be laid out in any prescriptive form. You will have to feel your way. In general, if you can think of an adjective to replace a noun used adjectivally, do so. You will hardly ever be wrong.

One last thing. It seems that only some teachers insist that their students speak clearly. Of course I mean *audibly* (audible speech from an American student these days is itself a welcome surprise). But even more urgently I mean *coherently*. What will happen if we allow the practitioners of the new grammarless grammar and expressionless expression to conquer a bit more of our linguistic earth? Perhaps we get a hint in Rachel Eve Glyn's response (in a 2006 letter to the *Wall Street Journal*) to an essay by Joseph Epstein.

> So Joseph Epstein's like, we oughta have a focus group to save the English language from, you know, going down the tubes, because we all know that bad English sucks. Wow, I mean, this dude is so totally cool in saying we don't talk right. So I'm like, we need to speak more clearly, but then society's like, never mind, do your own thing, whatever. If a person speaks correctly they sound more educated, but then other people go, like, you are some sort of snob or bigot.

Of course, Rachel Glyn is on *our* side, and does not herself practice such excess except in caustic imitation. Do people speak like that? I am afraid they do. And they write even more crudely. Can we all understand them? Well, er, it's like, I mean, y'know? Can we believe that people really want to represent themselves as ignorant and imprecise? Let's continue to hope not. This book is a gesture of solidarity with those who value clear expression.

What can we learn from thinking experimentally about grammar in relation to our own linguistic choices? It is surely less important to be "correct" than to know what we are doing as we use the full range of a language unusually various and (especially in America) compounded of so many diverse elements. It is no longer possible to maintain a strict obedience to Latin-based grammatical rules just because they governed our formal speech fifty or a hundred years ago. We need to consider their usefulness before we insist or even suggest that they be followed. I have tried to make a case for a conservative approach to traditional grammatical norms, arguing that they make our spoken or written expression stronger and clearer. Those who know why they speak and write as they do can be more effective in advancing their causes. The rest of us benefit from the growth of such powers in others.

PART IV: ANALYZING SENTENCES

A PARAGRAPH FROM THE WILD

While a few of the sample sentences in this little book have literary roots, most of them were made up to serve as examples. As a sort of graduation exercise, here are some sentences not bred in captivity for this grammatical zoo, but captured in the wild. They appear in a passage in *Madame Bovary* (1857), the much-admired novel by the French master Gustave Flaubert.

This little scene was written over a 150 years ago, but seems fresh as the morning it describes, with its first hint of spring. It presents (in my translation) Charles Bovary's fond vision of the woman he will eventually marry, with unhappy consequence.

> Once, during a thaw, the bark on the trees in the yard was dripping wet and the snow melted on the roofs of the buildings. She was standing at the threshold; she went back for her parasol; she opened it. The sunlight, passing through the iridescent silk, cast ripples of light over the white skin of her face. She was smiling at the mild

weather and drops of water were audible as they
fell, one after another, upon the taut silk.

There are four sentences here—let us consider them one
at a time.

The first sentence is *compound*, being made of two *independent clauses*: **Once, during a thaw, the bark on the trees
in the yard was dripping wet** and **the snow melted on the
roofs of the buildings.** The core of the first clause is formed
of its *subject and predicate*:

bark was

The writer adds a *predicate adjective* to describe the subject
whose state of being the verb *was* communicates:

bark was **wet**

A *present participle* acts like an adverb to modify the
adjective *wet*:

bark was **dripping** wet

A *prepositional phrase* (used *adjectivally*) describes the noun
bark:

The bark **on the trees** was dripping wet

Another *prepositional phrase* modifies *trees*:

The bark on the trees **in the yard** was dripping wet

An *adverb* and an *adverbial phrase* modify the verb *was*, establishing the time:

Once, during a thaw, the bark on the trees in the yard was dripping wet

We may apply the same technique to the second independent clause:

snow melted

the snow melted

the snow melted **on the roofs**

the snow melted on the roofs **of the buildings**

Finally, we join the two clauses with a *coordinating conjunction*:

Once, during a thaw, the bark on the trees in the yard was dripping wet **and** the snow melted on the roofs of the buildings.

The second sentence is formed of three *simple clauses* joined by semicolons: **She was standing at the threshold; she went back for her parasol; she opened it.** They show parallel construction—*she* begins each clause, and the first two clauses are parallel in inner construction, subject + verb + adverbial prepositional phrase.

She was

Add a participle used as a predicate adjective to describe what she was doing, or you could regard both words of *was standing* as constituting the verb in its past progressive form:

She was **standing**

Add a *prepositional phrase* to locate the action (either of the verb or the participial adjective) in space:

She was standing **at the threshold**

Second clause:

she went

Add an adverb modifying the verb:

she went **back**

Add a prepositional phrase:

she went back **for her parasol**

Third clause:

she opened

Add a pronoun (standing for the noun *parasol*) acting as a *direct object*, receiving the action of the transitive verb *opened*:

she opened **it**

The semicolons serve the same purpose as the coordinating conjunction *and*:

She was standing at the threshold; she went back for her parasol; she opened it.

The third sentence is a *simple sentence*, with four phrases along with its single clause: **The sunlight, passing through the iridescent silk, cast ripples of light over the white skin of her face.** As before, we begin with its core elements, the noun of the subject, the verb of the predicate:

sunlight cast

Add a direct object:

sunlight cast **ripples**

Then add two prepositional phrases to modify first *ripples*, then *light*:

sunlight cast ripples **of light over skin**

Then add a definite article, an adjective, and another prepositional phrase, all to modify the noun *skin*:

sunlight cast ripples of light over **the white** skin **of her face**

Then give the same treatment to *sunlight*—it is described by a participle:

The sunlight, **passing**

Add a prepositional phrase defining the place and action of the *passing*:

The sunlight, passing **through silk**

Add, finally, a definite article and an adjective to describe *silk*:

The sunlight, passing through **the iridescent** silk

Put it all together:

The sunlight, passing through the iridescent silk, cast ripples of light over the white skin of her face.

Finally, <u>the fourth sentence</u> is a *compound-complex sentence* with a *subordinate clause* in its second element: **She was smiling at the mild weather and drops of water were audible as they fell, one after another, upon the taut silk.** Take the core elements of the first clause:

She was

Add a predicate adjective to modify *she*. OR, as in the second sentence, take the verb and its participle, *was + smiling*, together as forming a past progressive form of the verb *to smile*:

She was **smiling**

Add a prepositional phrase:

She was smiling **at the weather**

Add an adjective modifying *weather*:

She was smiling at the **mild** weather

Take the core of the second clause:

drops were

Add a predicate adjective, describing the *drops*:

drops were **audible**

Then add an adjectival prepositional phrase, again describing the drops:

drops **of water** were audible

Add a subordinate clause used adverbially to set the time for the core predicate *were audible*:

drops of water were audible **as they fell**

(*They* is the subject of the clause and *fell* its predicate; *as* is a temporal subordinating conjunction.)

Add two adverbial phrases modifying *fell*:

drops of water were audible as they fell, **one after another, upon the silk**

Add an adjective modifying *silk*:

drops of water were audible as they fell, one after another, upon the **taut** silk

Finally, a coordinating conjunction unites the clauses:

She was smiling at the mild weather **and** drops of water were audible as they fell, one after another, upon the taut silk.

There are many points in the above parsing that grammarians might fairly dispute among themselves. For example, I suggested two views of *smiling* in the last sentence—it could be a participle acting as a predicate adjective modifying *she*, or it could be part of a past progressive verb form *was smiling*. Moreover, if you regard *smiling* as a part of a compound verb *to smile at*, then *weather* becomes its direct object and not part of a prepositional phrase.

Such definitional debates make people despair of grammar (and of grammarians). They are fun for *aficionados*, but do not matter much to most people. Such parsings as these are not primarily useful as a search for "truth," but as a way to encounter the elements of a sentence and discern its construction. I used to tell students that there are things we must learn in order to have a basic discussion of some interesting issues. Learning them is difficult, but our reward is that once we have mastered the concepts involved, we never need to study them again—we will have made them parts of ourselves. Does it really matter whether *at the weather* is or is not a genuine prepositional phrase? Or whether *to smile at* is or is not a genuine verb? I do not believe it does.

Interesting as these points may be to specialists, and to those who admire and enjoy theoretical discussions, I think the rest of us should give over debating such issues. All that matters is that we have confidence in the linguistic competence of the person to whom we are lending our attention. We do not need to parse every sentence we read or hear. It is enough that we have a strong sense that what Flaubert is saying is comprehensible and that we are equipped to understand his words and their relationships one to another. Affixing labels to them is not our primary concern.

Diagramming sentences

When I was growing up grammar was taught, earnestly and rigorously, to most schoolchildren (if not to me). A technique then in widespread use, but now almost wholly forgotten, was *diagramming sentences*. Sentences were analyzed more or less as we have just done with the passage from Flaubert. Then the words were connected by lines indicating the grammatical function of each element of the sentence. Here is one of Flaubert's sentences, used as an example:

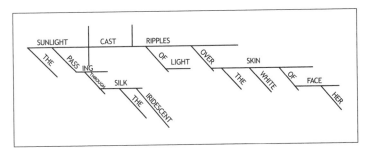

This technique, called *Reed-Kellogg diagramming* and traceable to the nineteenth century, was a powerful teaching method, one that happens to be fun to use. Capital Community College of Hartford, Connecticut has laid out the elements of this useful and entertaining system on its website at

http://grammar.ccc.commnet.edu/grammar/diagrams/diagrams.htm

Additional linked pages show the conventions for dozens of grammatical forms. The method is well worth reviving.

INDEX OF TERMS

adjectives, 20–23
    comparative forms of, 21
    limiting or qualitative, 21

adverbs, 23–24
    comparative forms of, 23–24

agreement, 41–51
    case, 42–43
    number, 41
    gender, 41–42

articles, 22–23
    definite or indefinite, 22

as or like?, 65–66

barbarism, 40

because of or due to?, 67–69

between or among?, 66–67

clause, 37
    dependent, 37
    independent, 37

conjugation, 15–17

conjunctions, 24–27
   coordinating, 24
   correlative, 25
   subordinating, 25
   temporal, causal, concessive, conditional, 26–27

discourse, levels of, 58–74

due to or because of?, 67–69

infinitives, 32–33
   split, 51–55

interjections, 28–29

like or as?, 65–66

noun (*nomen*), 12–13
   collective, 44–46

object, 35–36
   direct, 36
   indirect, 36
   of a preposition, 36

participle, 29–30
   dangling, 30

predicate, 35

preposition and prepositional phrases, 27–28
   dangling, 71–72

pronoun, 12–14
   "hef", 50

    hir, 50

    interrogative, 13

    reflexive, 13

    relative, 13

proper noun, 12

sentence, 34–39

    complex, 37–38

    compound, 37–38

    compound-complex, 37–38

    fragmentary, 38

solecism, 40

style, 58–62

subject, 35–36

subjunctive mood, 55–58

that or which?, 69–71

usage, 40–74

verbals, 29–33

    participles, 29–30

    gerunds, 31

    infinitives, 32–33

verbs, 15–20

    active or passive, 15

    of action, 15

    of state, 15

which or that?, 69–71

who or whom?, 62–65

APPENDIX

See page 92 for the answers.

EXERCISE 1: Kinds of Clauses

Each of the following sentences contains at least two clauses. Which of them is independent? Which dependent?

(1) Dante's *Divine Comedy* is a poem; it is in three parts.

(2) Whether or not one likes it, one must admit that it is impressive.

(3) Its cast of characters is enormous and its variety of setting is, too.

(4) Because I enjoy so many characters, it is difficult to say which one is my favorite.

(5) If you had to pick two, I bet that they would include Francesca and Ulysses.

(6) I am less conventional than you are; my choice is Cato and Piccarda.

(7) Don't you find that such discussions verge on the banal?

(8) Who are you that you feel free to ask such hostile questions?

EXERCISE 2: Agreement (case, number, gender)

In each of the following sentences choose the correct form of the pronoun or pronominal adjective.

(1) Someone had forgotten (*their* or *his or her*) bookbag in the car.

(2) Did she think it was (*he* or *him*)?

(3) Shall we ask the members of the board for (*their* or *its*) opinion?

(4) The board might take any number of positions. What do we expect of (*it* or *them*)?

(5) David is not a person (*who* or *whom*) it is easy to like.

(6) On the other hand, he seems the kind of man (*who* or *whom*) admires others.

(7) I happen to know a person (*who* or *whom*) David really liked.

(8) Perhaps those who think ill of him need to rethink (*his or her* or *their*) view.

EXERCISE 3: The Subjunctive

Choose the correct form of the verb in each of the following sentences:

(1) If I (*were* or *was*) king, I would free all those jailed for singing too loud.

(2) (*Were* or *Was*) you to make a similar decision, you wouldn't be re-elected.

(3) Whatever she (*choose* or *chooses*), I would fight for her right to do so.

(4) Whatever she (*had* or *has*) done, I would have supported her.

(5) I would never support a candidate who (*had* or *has*) demonstrated so little energy.

(6) It is not our wish that our members (*support* or *supported*) any one view.

(7) I wish that the committee (*has* or *had*) considered those details carefully.

(8) (*Were* or *Was*) she capable of committing such an act, she never would have said so.

Exercise 4: *like* or *as?*

*Choose between **like** and **as** in each of the following sentences:*

(1) A president should always try to avoid behaving (*as* or *like*) a politician.

(2) (*As* or *Like*) presidents, they never even seemed to be politicians.

(3) I have become far more tolerant, (*as* or *like*) you can see.

(4) Are you qualified (*as* or *like*) an electrician?

(5) She joined that terrible firm (*as* or *like*) director of good will.

(6) He was fuming, just (*as* or *like*) a fool in an old cartoon.

(7) Behaving (*as* or *like*) a madman, he lost control.

(8) If we are going to make that meeting, we need to run (*as* or *like*) the wind.

EXERCISE 5: *between* or *among*?

*Choose **between** or **among** in each of the following sentences:*

(1) She was pleased to find herself seated (*between* or *among*) the most senior members of the faculty.

(2) He found himself seated on the bench (*between* or *among*) the Dean of the Chapel and her burly assistant.

(3) He thus found himself (*between* or *among*) the Dean, a rock, and a hard place.

(4) (*Between* or *Among*) us, all members of this squad, let there be no enmity.

(5) (*Between* or *Among*) us, the two youngest members, let there be friendship.

(6) Who can possibly choose (*between* or *among*) so many positive options?

(7) There is no such thing as honor (*between* or *among*) thieves.

(8) There is, at least (*between* or *among*) the two of us, decency and even friendship.

EXERCISE 6: *due to* or *because of*?

*Choose between **due to** or **because of** in each of the following sentences:*

(1) (*Due to* or *Because of*) the length of the performance, Gwyneth was exhausted.

(2) Her exhilaration was (*due to* or *because of*) the audience's enthusiastic response.

(3) She had to ask the stage manager to open the curtain (*due to* or *because of*) the prolonged applause.

(4) "My achievement," she said, "is entirely (*due to* or *because of*) my father's patience, if possibly also a bit (*due to* or *because of*) his wealth."

(5) (*Due to* or *Because of*) her wounded ego, she waltzed away with Hugo.

(6) He was turning heads (*due to* or *because of*) his easy manner and startling good looks.

(7) (*Due to* or *Because of*) her intense involvement in charity work, she ended up canceling her weekly game of tennis.

(8) Whatever happiness she enjoyed was (*due to* or *because of*) her involvement in good works for the benefit of others.

ANSWERS

Exercise 1: Kinds of Clauses
1. I/I; 2. D/I; 3. I/I; 4. D/I/D; 5. D/I/D; 6. I/D/I; 7. I/D; 8. I/D.

Exercise 2: Agreement (case, number, gender)
1. his or her; 2. he; 3. their; 4. it *or* them; 5. whom; 6. who; 7. whom; 8. their.

Exercise 3: The Subjunctive
1. were; 2. Were; 3. choose; 4. had; 5. had; 6. support; 7. had; 8. Were.

Exercise 4: *like* or *as*?
1, 6, 7, 8: like; 2, 3, 4, 5: as.

Exercise 5: *between* or *among*?
1, 3, 4, 6, 7: among; 2, 5, 8: between.

Exercise 6: *due to* or *because of*?
1, 3, 5, 6, 7: because of; 2, 4, 8: due to.

A CATALOG OF SELECTED DOVER BOOKS IN ALL FIELDS OF INTEREST

100 BEST-LOVED POEMS, Edited by Philip Smith. "The Passionate Shepherd to His Love," "Shall I compare thee to a summer's day?" "Death, be not proud," "The Raven," "The Road Not Taken," plus works by Blake, Wordsworth, Byron, Shelley, Keats, many others. 96pp. 5³⁄₁₆ x 8¼.   0-486-28553-7

100 SMALL HOUSES OF THE THIRTIES, Brown-Blodgett Company. Exterior photographs and floor plans for 100 charming structures. Illustrations of models accompanied by descriptions of interiors, color schemes, closet space, and other amenities. 200 illustrations. 112pp. 8⅜ x 11.   0-486-44131-8

1000 TURN-OF-THE-CENTURY HOUSES: With Illustrations and Floor Plans, Herbert C. Chivers. Reproduced from a rare edition, this showcase of homes ranges from cottages and bungalows to sprawling mansions. Each house is meticulously illustrated and accompanied by complete floor plans. 256pp. 9⅜ x 12¼.
0-486-45596-3

101 GREAT AMERICAN POEMS, Edited by The American Poetry & Literacy Project. Rich treasury of verse from the 19th and 20th centuries includes works by Edgar Allan Poe, Robert Frost, Walt Whitman, Langston Hughes, Emily Dickinson, T. S. Eliot, other notables. 96pp. 5³⁄₁₆ x 8¼.   0-486-40158-8

101 GREAT SAMURAI PRINTS, Utagawa Kuniyoshi. Kuniyoshi was a master of the warrior woodblock print — and these 18th-century illustrations represent the pinnacle of his craft. Full-color portraits of renowned Japanese samurais pulse with movement, passion, and remarkably fine detail. 112pp. 8⅜ x 11.
0-486-46523-3

ABC OF BALLET, Janet Grosser. Clearly worded, abundantly illustrated little guide defines basic ballet-related terms: arabesque, battement, pas de chat, relevé, sissonne, many others. Pronunciation guide included. Excellent primer. 48pp. 4³⁄₁₆ x 5¾.   0-486-40871-X

ACCESSORIES OF DRESS: An Illustrated Encyclopedia, Katherine Lester and Bess Viola Oerke. Illustrations of hats, veils, wigs, cravats, shawls, shoes, gloves, and other accessories enhance an engaging commentary that reveals the humor and charm of the many-sided story of accessorized apparel. 644 figures and 59 plates. 608pp. 6⅛ x 9¼.   0-486-43378-1

ADVENTURES OF HUCKLEBERRY FINN, Mark Twain. Join Huck and Jim as their boyhood adventures along the Mississippi River lead them into a world of excitement, danger, and self-discovery. Humorous narrative, lyrical descriptions of the Mississippi valley, and memorable characters. 224pp. 5³⁄₁₆ x 8¼. 0-486-28061-6

Browse over 9,000 books at www.doverpublications.com

ALICE STARMORE'S BOOK OF FAIR ISLE KNITTING, Alice Starmore. A noted designer from the region of Scotland's Fair Isle explores the history and techniques of this distinctive, stranded-color knitting style and provides copious illustrated instructions for 14 original knitwear designs. 208pp. 8⅜ x 10⅞.
0-486-47218-3

ALICE'S ADVENTURES IN WONDERLAND, Lewis Carroll. Beloved classic about a little girl lost in a topsy-turvy land and her encounters with the White Rabbit, March Hare, Mad Hatter, Cheshire Cat, and other delightfully improbable characters. 42 illustrations by Sir John Tenniel. 96pp. 5³⁄₁₆ x 8¼.
0-486-27543-4

AMERICA'S LIGHTHOUSES: An Illustrated History, Francis Ross Holland. Profusely illustrated fact-filled survey of American lighthouses since 1716. Over 200 stations — East, Gulf, and West coasts, Great Lakes, Hawaii, Alaska, Puerto Rico, the Virgin Islands, and the Mississippi and St. Lawrence Rivers. 240pp. 8 x 10¾.
0-486-25576-X

AN ENCYCLOPEDIA OF THE VIOLIN, Alberto Bachmann. Translated by Frederick H. Martens. Introduction by Eugene Ysaye. First published in 1925, this renowned reference remains unsurpassed as a source of essential information, from construction and evolution to repertoire and technique. Includes a glossary and 73 illustrations. 496pp. 6⅛ x 9¼.
0-486-46618-3

ANIMALS: 1,419 Copyright-Free Illustrations of Mammals, Birds, Fish, Insects, etc., Selected by Jim Harter. Selected for its visual impact and ease of use, this outstanding collection of wood engravings presents over 1,000 species of animals in extremely lifelike poses. Includes mammals, birds, reptiles, amphibians, fish, insects, and other invertebrates. 284pp. 9 x 12.
0-486-23766-4

THE ANNALS, Tacitus. Translated by Alfred John Church and William Jackson Brodribb. This vital chronicle of Imperial Rome, written by the era's great historian, spans A.D. 14-68 and paints incisive psychological portraits of major figures, from Tiberius to Nero. 416pp. 5³⁄₁₆ x 8¼.
0-486-45236-0

ANTIGONE, Sophocles. Filled with passionate speeches and sensitive probing of moral and philosophical issues, this powerful and often-performed Greek drama reveals the grim fate that befalls the children of Oedipus. Footnotes. 64pp. 5³⁄₁₆ x 8 ¼.
0-486-27804-2

ART DECO DECORATIVE PATTERNS IN FULL COLOR, Christian Stoll. Reprinted from a rare 1910 portfolio, 160 sensuous and exotic images depict a breathtaking array of florals, geometrics, and abstracts — all elegant in their stark simplicity. 64pp. 8⅜ x 11.
0-486-44862-2

Browse over 9,000 books at www.doverpublications.com

THE ARTHUR RACKHAM TREASURY: 86 Full-Color Illustrations, Arthur Rackham. Selected and Edited by Jeff A. Menges. A stunning treasury of 86 full-page plates span the famed English artist's career, from *Rip Van Winkle* (1905) to masterworks such as *Undine, A Midsummer Night's Dream,* and *Wind in the Willows* (1939). 96pp. 8⅜ x 11.   0-486-44685-9

THE AUTHENTIC GILBERT & SULLIVAN SONGBOOK, W. S. Gilbert and A. S. Sullivan. The most comprehensive collection available, this songbook includes selections from every one of Gilbert and Sullivan's light operas. Ninety-two numbers are presented uncut and unedited, and in their original keys. 410pp. 9 x 12.   0-486-23482-7

THE AWAKENING, Kate Chopin. First published in 1899, this controversial novel of a New Orleans wife's search for love outside a stifling marriage shocked readers. Today, it remains a first-rate narrative with superb characterization. New introductory Note. 128pp. 5³⁄₁₆ x 8¼.   0-486-27786-0

BASIC DRAWING, Louis Priscilla. Beginning with perspective, this common-sense manual progresses to the figure in movement, light and shade, anatomy, drapery, composition, trees and landscape, and outdoor sketching. Black-and-white illustrations throughout. 128pp. 8⅜ x 11.   0-486-45815-6

THE BATTLES THAT CHANGED HISTORY, Fletcher Pratt. Historian profiles 16 crucial conflicts, ancient to modern, that changed the course of Western civilization. Gripping accounts of battles led by Alexander the Great, Joan of Arc, Ulysses S. Grant, other commanders. 27 maps. 352pp. 5⅜ x 8½.   0-486-41129-X

BEETHOVEN'S LETTERS, Ludwig van Beethoven. Edited by Dr. A. C. Kalischer. Features 457 letters to fellow musicians, friends, greats, patrons, and literary men. Reveals musical thoughts, quirks of personality, insights, and daily events. Includes 15 plates. 410pp. 5⅜ x 8½.   0-486-22769-3

BERNICE BOBS HER HAIR AND OTHER STORIES, F. Scott Fitzgerald. This brilliant anthology includes 6 of Fitzgerald's most popular stories: "The Diamond as Big as the Ritz," the title tale, "The Offshore Pirate," "The Ice Palace," "The Jelly Bean," and "May Day." 176pp. 5⅜ x 8½.   0-486-47049-0

BESLER'S BOOK OF FLOWERS AND PLANTS: 73 Full-Color Plates from Hortus Eystettensis, 1613, Basilius Besler. Here is a selection of magnificent plates from the *Hortus Eystettensis,* which vividly illustrated and identified the plants, flowers, and trees that thrived in the legendary German garden at Eichstätt. 80pp. 8⅜ x 11.   0-486-46005-3

THE BOOK OF KELLS, Edited by Blanche Cirker. Painstakingly reproduced from a rare facsimile edition, this volume contains full-page decorations, portraits, illustrations, plus a sampling of textual leaves with exquisite calligraphy and ornamentation. 32 full-color illustrations. 32pp. 9⅜ x 12¼.   0-486-24345-1

THE BOOK OF THE CROSSBOW: With an Additional Section on Catapults and Other Siege Engines, Ralph Payne-Gallwey. Fascinating study traces history and use of crossbow as military and sporting weapon, from Middle Ages to modern times. Also covers related weapons: balistas, catapults, Turkish bows, more. Over 240 illustrations. 400pp. 7¼ x 10⅛.   0-486-28720-3

THE BUNGALOW BOOK: Floor Plans and Photos of 112 Houses, 1910, Henry L. Wilson. Here are 112 of the most popular and economic blueprints of the early 20th century — plus an illustration or photograph of each completed house. A wonderful time capsule that still offers a wealth of valuable insights. 160pp. 8⅜ x 11   0-486-45104-6

THE CALL OF THE WILD, Jack London. A classic novel of adventure, drawn from London's own experiences as a Klondike adventurer, relating the story of a heroic dog caught in the brutal life of the Alaska Gold Rush. Note. 64pp. 5³⁄₁₆ x 8¼.   0-486-26472-6

CANDIDE, Voltaire. Edited by Francois-Marie Arouet. One of the world's great satires since its first publication in 1759. Witty, caustic skewering of romance, science, philosophy, religion, government — nearly all human ideals and institutions. 112pp. 5³⁄₁₆ x 8¼.   0-486-26689-3

CELEBRATED IN THEIR TIME: Photographic Portraits from the George Grantham Bain Collection, Edited by Amy Pastan. With an Introduction by Michael Carlebach. Remarkable portrait gallery features 112 rare images of Albert Einstein, Charlie Chaplin, the Wright Brothers, Henry Ford, and other luminaries from the worlds of politics, art, entertainment, and industry. 128pp. 8⅜ x 11.   0-486-46754-6

CHARIOTS FOR APOLLO: The NASA History of Manned Lunar Spacecraft to 1969, Courtney G. Brooks, James M. Grimwood, and Loyd S. Swenson, Jr. This illustrated history by a trio of experts is the definitive reference on the Apollo spacecraft and lunar modules. It traces the vehicles' design, development, and operation in space. More than 100 photographs and illustrations. 576pp. 6¾ x 9¼.   0-486-46756-2

A CHRISTMAS CAROL, Charles Dickens. This engrossing tale relates Ebenezer Scrooge's ghostly journeys through Christmases past, present, and future and his ultimate transformation from a harsh and grasping old miser to a charitable and compassionate human being. 80pp. 5³⁄₁₆ x 8¼.   0-486-26865-9

COMMON SENSE, Thomas Paine. First published in January of 1776, this highly influential landmark document clearly and persuasively argued for American separation from Great Britain and paved the way for the Declaration of Independence. 64pp. 5³⁄₁₆ x 8¼.   0-486-29602-4

THE COMPLETE SHORT STORIES OF OSCAR WILDE, Oscar Wilde. Complete texts of "The Happy Prince and Other Tales," "A House of Pomegranates," "Lord Arthur Savile's Crime and Other Stories," "Poems in Prose," and "The Portrait of Mr. W. H." 208pp. 5³⁄₁₆ x 8¼. 0-486-45216-6

COMPLETE SONNETS, William Shakespeare. Over 150 exquisite poems deal with love, friendship, the tyranny of time, beauty's evanescence, death, and other themes in language of remarkable power, precision, and beauty. Glossary of archaic terms. 80pp. 5³⁄₁₆ x 8¼. 0-486-26686-9

THE COUNT OF MONTE CRISTO: Abridged Edition, Alexandre Dumas. Falsely accused of treason, Edmond Dantès is imprisoned in the bleak Chateau d'If. After a hair-raising escape, he launches an elaborate plot to extract a bitter revenge against those who betrayed him. 448pp. 5³⁄₁₆ x 8¼. 0-486-45643-9

CRAFTSMAN BUNGALOWS: Designs from the Pacific Northwest, Yoho & Merritt. This reprint of a rare catalog, showcasing the charming simplicity and cozy style of Craftsman bungalows, is filled with photos of completed homes, plus floor plans and estimated costs. An indispensable resource for architects, historians, and illustrators. 112pp. 10 x 7. 0-486-46875-5

CRAFTSMAN BUNGALOWS: 59 Homes from "The Craftsman," Edited by Gustav Stickley. Best and most attractive designs from Arts and Crafts Movement publication — 1903–1916 — includes sketches, photographs of homes, floor plans, descriptive text. 128pp. 8¼ x 11. 0-486-25829-7

CRIME AND PUNISHMENT, Fyodor Dostoyevsky. Translated by Constance Garnett. Supreme masterpiece tells the story of Raskolnikov, a student tormented by his own thoughts after he murders an old woman. Overwhelmed by guilt and terror, he confesses and goes to prison. 480pp. 5³⁄₁₆ x 8¼. 0-486-41587-2

THE DECLARATION OF INDEPENDENCE AND OTHER GREAT DOCUMENTS OF AMERICAN HISTORY: 1775-1865, Edited by John Grafton. Thirteen compelling and influential documents: Henry's "Give Me Liberty or Give Me Death," Declaration of Independence, The Constitution, Washington's First Inaugural Address, The Monroe Doctrine, The Emancipation Proclamation, Gettysburg Address, more. 64pp. 5³⁄₁₆ x 8¼. 0-486-41124-9

THE DESERT AND THE SOWN: Travels in Palestine and Syria, Gertrude Bell. "The female Lawrence of Arabia," Gertrude Bell wrote captivating, perceptive accounts of her travels in the Middle East. This intriguing narrative, accompanied by 160 photos, traces her 1905 sojourn in Lebanon, Syria, and Palestine. 368pp. 5⅜ x 8½. 0-486-46876-3

Browse over 9,000 books at www.doverpublications.com

A DOLL'S HOUSE, Henrik Ibsen. Ibsen's best-known play displays his genius for realistic prose drama. An expression of women's rights, the play climaxes when the central character, Nora, rejects a smothering marriage and life in "a doll's house." 80pp. 5³⁄₁₆ x 8¼. 0-486-27062-9

DOOMED SHIPS: Great Ocean Liner Disasters, William H. Miller, Jr. Nearly 200 photographs, many from private collections, highlight tales of some of the vessels whose pleasure cruises ended in catastrophe: the *Morro Castle, Normandie, Andrea Doria, Europa,* and many others. 128pp. 8⅞ x 11¾. 0-486-45366-9

THE DORÉ BIBLE ILLUSTRATIONS, Gustave Doré. Detailed plates from the Bible: the Creation scenes, Adam and Eve, horrifying visions of the Flood, the battle sequences with their monumental crowds, depictions of the life of Jesus, 241 plates in all. 241pp. 9 x 12. 0-486-23004-X

DRAWING DRAPERY FROM HEAD TO TOE, Cliff Young. Expert guidance on how to draw shirts, pants, skirts, gloves, hats, and coats on the human figure, including folds in relation to the body, pull and crush, action folds, creases, more. Over 200 drawings. 48pp. 8¼ x 11. 0-486-45591-2

DUBLINERS, James Joyce. A fine and accessible introduction to the work of one of the 20th century's most influential writers, this collection features 15 tales, including a masterpiece of the short-story genre, "The Dead." 160pp. 5³⁄₁₆ x 8¼. 0-486-26870-5

EASY-TO-MAKE POP-UPS, Joan Irvine. Illustrated by Barbara Reid. Dozens of wonderful ideas for three-dimensional paper fun — from holiday greeting cards with moving parts to a pop-up menagerie. Easy-to-follow, illustrated instructions for more than 30 projects. 299 black-and-white illustrations. 96pp. 8⅞ x 11. 0-486-44622-0

EASY-TO-MAKE STORYBOOK DOLLS: A "Novel" Approach to Cloth Dollmaking, Sherralyn St. Clair. Favorite fictional characters come alive in this unique beginner's dollmaking guide. Includes patterns for Pollyanna, Dorothy from *The Wonderful Wizard of Oz,* Mary of *The Secret Garden,* plus easy-to-follow instructions, 263 black-and-white illustrations, and an 8-page color insert. 112pp. 8¼ x 11. 0-486-47360-0

EINSTEIN'S ESSAYS IN SCIENCE, Albert Einstein. Speeches and essays in accessible, everyday language profile influential physicists such as Niels Bohr and Isaac Newton. They also explore areas of physics to which the author made major contributions. 128pp. 5 x 8. 0-486-47011-3

EL DORADO: Further Adventures of the Scarlet Pimpernel, Baroness Orczy. A popular sequel to *The Scarlet Pimpernel,* this suspenseful story recounts the Pimpernel's attempts to rescue the Dauphin from imprisonment during the French Revolution. An irresistible blend of intrigue, period detail, and vibrant characterizations. 352pp. 5³⁄₁₆ x 8¼. 0-486-44026-5

ELEGANT SMALL HOMES OF THE TWENTIES: 99 Designs from a Competition, Chicago Tribune. Nearly 100 designs for five- and six-room houses feature New England and Southern colonials, Normandy cottages, stately Italianate dwellings, and other fascinating snapshots of American domestic architecture of the 1920s. 112pp. 9 x 12.   0-486-46910-7

THE ELEMENTS OF STYLE: The Original Edition, William Strunk, Jr. This is the book that generations of writers have relied upon for timeless advice on grammar, diction, syntax, and other essentials. In concise terms, it identifies the principal requirements of proper style and common errors. 64pp. 5⅜ x 8½.   0-486-44798-7

THE ELUSIVE PIMPERNEL, Baroness Orczy. Robespierre's revolutionaries find their wicked schemes thwarted by the heroic Pimpernel — Sir Percival Blakeney. In this thrilling sequel, Chauvelin devises a plot to eliminate the Pimpernel and his wife. 272pp. 5³⁄₁₆ x 8¼.   0-486-45464-9

AN ENCYCLOPEDIA OF BATTLES: Accounts of Over 1,560 Battles from 1479 B.C. to the Present, David Eggenberger. Essential details of every major battle in recorded history from the first battle of Megiddo in 1479 B.C. to Grenada in 1984. List of battle maps. 99 illustrations. 544pp. 6½ x 9¼.   0-486-24913-1

ENCYCLOPEDIA OF EMBROIDERY STITCHES, INCLUDING CREWEL, Marion Nichols. Precise explanations and instructions, clearly illustrated, on how to work chain, back, cross, knotted, woven stitches, and many more — 178 in all, including Cable Outline, Whipped Satin, and Eyelet Buttonhole. Over 1400 illustrations. 219pp. 8⅜ x 11¼.   0-486-22929-7

ENTER JEEVES: 15 Early Stories, P. G. Wodehouse. Splendid collection contains first 8 stories featuring Bertie Wooster, the deliciously dim aristocrat and Jeeves, his brainy, imperturbable manservant. Also, the complete Reggie Pepper (Bertie's prototype) series. 288pp. 5⅜ x 8½.   0-486-29717-9

ERIC SLOANE'S AMERICA: Paintings in Oil, Michael Wigley. With a Foreword by Mimi Sloane. Eric Sloane's evocative oils of America's landscape and material culture shimmer with immense historical and nostalgic appeal. This original hardcover collection gathers nearly a hundred of his finest paintings, with subjects ranging from New England to the American Southwest. 128pp. 10⅜ x 9.   0-486-46525-X

ETHAN FROME, Edith Wharton. Classic story of wasted lives, set against a bleak New England background. Superbly delineated characters in a hauntingly grim tale of thwarted love. Considered by many to be Wharton's masterpiece. 96pp. 5³⁄₁₆ x 8 ¼.   0-486-26690-7

THE EVERLASTING MAN, G. K. Chesterton. Chesterton's view of Christianity — as a blend of philosophy and mythology, satisfying intellect and spirit — applies to his brilliant book, which appeals to readers' heads as well as their hearts. 288pp. 5⅜ x 8½.   0-486-46036-3

Browse over 9,000 books at www.doverpublications.com

THE FIELD AND FOREST HANDY BOOK, Daniel Beard. Written by a co-founder of the Boy Scouts, this appealing guide offers illustrated instructions for building kites, birdhouses, boats, igloos, and other fun projects, plus numerous helpful tips for campers. 448pp. 5³⁄₁₆ x 8¼. 0-486-46191-2

FINDING YOUR WAY WITHOUT MAP OR COMPASS, Harold Gatty. Useful, instructive manual shows would-be explorers, hikers, bikers, scouts, sailors, and survivalists how to find their way outdoors by observing animals, weather patterns, shifting sands, and other elements of nature. 288pp. 5⅜ x 8½. 0-486-40613-X

FIRST FRENCH READER: A Beginner's Dual-Language Book, Edited and Translated by Stanley Appelbaum. This anthology introduces 50 legendary writers — Voltaire, Balzac, Baudelaire, Proust, more — through passages from *The Red and the Black, Les Misérables, Madame Bovary,* and other classics. Original French text plus English translation on facing pages. 240pp. 5⅜ x 8½. 0-486-46178-5

FIRST GERMAN READER: A Beginner's Dual-Language Book, Edited by Harry Steinhauer. Specially chosen for their power to evoke German life and culture, these short, simple readings include poems, stories, essays, and anecdotes by Goethe, Hesse, Heine, Schiller, and others. 224pp. 5⅜ x 8½. 0-486-46179-3

FIRST SPANISH READER: A Beginner's Dual-Language Book, Angel Flores. Delightful stories, other material based on works of Don Juan Manuel, Luis Taboada, Ricardo Palma, other noted writers. Complete faithful English translations on facing pages. Exercises. 176pp. 5⅜ x 8½. 0-486-25810-6

FIVE ACRES AND INDEPENDENCE, Maurice G. Kains. Great back-to-the-land classic explains basics of self-sufficient farming. The one book to get. 95 illustrations. 397pp. 5⅜ x 8½. 0-486-20974-1

FLAGG'S SMALL HOUSES: Their Economic Design and Construction, 1922, Ernest Flagg. Although most famous for his skyscrapers, Flagg was also a proponent of the well-designed single-family dwelling. His classic treatise features innovations that save space, materials, and cost. 526 illustrations. 160pp. 9⅜ x 12¼. 0-486-45197-6

FLATLAND: A Romance of Many Dimensions, Edwin A. Abbott. Classic of science (and mathematical) fiction — charmingly illustrated by the author — describes the adventures of A. Square, a resident of Flatland, in Spaceland (three dimensions), Lineland (one dimension), and Pointland (no dimensions). 96pp. 5³⁄₁₆ x 8¼. 0-486-27263-X

Browse over 9,000 books at www.doverpublications.com